0 × (10/10)

1 ✗ 3/11 10

LO

skeptical chemist:

the story of

Robert Boyle

skeptical chemist:
the story of

Robert Boyle

Roberta Baxter

MORGAN
REYNOLDS

PUBLISHING

Greensboro, North Carolina

Profiles
IN SCIENCE

Robert Boyle
Rosalind Franklin
Ibn al-Haytham
Edmond Halley
Marie Curie
Antonio Meucci
Caroline Herschel

SKEPTICAL CHEMIST: THE STORY OF ROBERT BOYLE

Copyright © 2006 by Roberta Baxter

Library of Congress Cataloging-in-Publication Data

Baxter, Roberta, 1952-
  Skeptical chemist : the story of Robert Boyle / by Roberta Baxter.
    p. cm.
  Includes bibliographical references and index.
  ISBN-13: 978-1-59935-025-7 (library binding)
  ISBN-10: 1-59935-025-4 (library binding)
  1. Boyle, Robert, 1627-1691. 2. Scientists--Great
Britain--Biography--Juvenile literature. I. Title.
Q143.B77B39 2006
509.2--dc22
[B]
                                        2006023969

Printed in the United States of America
First Edition

contents

Robert Boyle. (Courtesy of the Granger Collection.)

ONE

privileged son

On the morning of August 30, 1658, the natural philosopher and gentleman Robert Boyle awoke, went to his laboratory, and took the readings on several of his instruments. The instrument that most interested him on this day was the barometer, which had been invented less than twenty years before.

A barometer measures the weight, or pressure, of the atmosphere, and Boyle was convinced a barometer could predict the weather. Based on his previous observations, it seemed that lower pressure indicated an approaching storm and higher pressure meant that fairer weather was on the way.

When Boyle checked the barometer reading that August morning, it registered the lowest pressure he had ever seen. If he was right, this meant a violent storm was approaching.

Unfortunately, he was right. In a short time a tempest descended upon England that became a legend. People cowered in their homes as winds ripped off roofs and uprooted trees.

Only three days after the storm, England's Lord Protector, Oliver Cromwell, died of malaria. Some claimed the tempest had been an omen of his impending death. Robert Boyle, on the other hand, was certain that the barometer had predicted the storm, and his certainty was based on measurement and observation, not on omens. Boyle was not the first to observe that barometers predict the weather, but his insistence on rigorous, scientific thinking singled him out in an age when many still clung to superstitions and dogma.

Robert Boyle was born on January 25, 1627, at Lismore Castle, which was perched above the Blackwater River in the southern Irish province of Munster. The castle and its surrounding lands was only one of several estates that Robert's father, Richard Boyle, the First Earl of Cork, had bought from the English writer and explorer Sir Walter Raleigh twenty-five years before. At the time of his son's birth, Richard Boyle was the wealthiest man in the British Isles, but he had not started out rich. Richard was born into a respected but poor family in Kent, England, in 1566 and, at the age of twenty-two, had set off to seek his fortune in Ireland with only twenty-six pounds, a few valuables, and the clothes on his back.

Once in Ireland, Richard Boyle married a wealthy heiress, who died in childbirth and left him an estate and a yearly

Robert Boyle's birthplace, Lismore Castle in Munster, Ireland, was once owned by the explorer and writer Sir Walter Raleigh. (British Library)

income he used to invest in the iron industry and to buy land and castles. After amassing one of the biggest domains in Ireland, he was knighted in 1603 and became the First Earl of Cork, a peerage that still exists. In an autobiography, written when he was in his twenties, Robert Boyle said of his father, he, "by God's blessing on his prosperous industry, from very inconsiderable beginnings, built so plentiful and so eminent a fortune, that his prosperity has found many admirers, but few parallels."

On the same day he was knighted, Richard married Robert's mother, Catherine Fenton, the daughter of an Irish noble. They had fifteen children, twelve of whom lived to be adults; Robert was the fourteenth. Richard enthusiastically set about strategically marrying off his children to enhance his own power and connections.

Although Richard Boyle expected one of his sons to carry on his legacy, Robert, being the youngest, was spared the

Robert's father, Richard Boyle, First Earl of Cork. (The Earl of Cork and Orrery)

constant grooming Richard performed on his older sons. "To be such parents' son and not their eldest," Robert later wrote of his childhood, "was a Happiness that [I] would mention with great expressions of gratitude." Robert could enjoy the comforts of wealth without the responsibilities of power. He was also said to be his father's favorite.

Richard Boyle did not want his sons to be spoiled by wealth. "Great men's children breeding up at home tempts them to nicety, to pride, and idleness, and contributes much more to give them a good opinion of themselves, than to make them deserve it," Robert later observed. As soon as Robert was old enough to leave his mother, he was sent to live with a peasant family for the first years of his life and did not return to Lismore Castle until he was four. While he was gone, his mother Catherine died of tuberculosis. Robert never knew her.

Though Richard's intention in sending his sons away was to make them hardier, Robert was a shy and mild boy. At a young age, he developed a severe stutter that plagued him all his life. He believed it was God's punishment for an incident when he had teased another child who stuttered. Robert was uneasy in social situations and an outsider to his friends and peers. But his father adored him and praised his kindness and honesty—traits Robert's admirers would cite throughout his life. One time, when Robert's sister Katherine scolded him for eating six plums he was not supposed to have eaten, Robert answered that it had actually been "half a score," or ten plums.

Robert was brought up to be intensely religious. The earl

was a member of the Church of England, also known as the Anglican Church. During the 1600s much of Europe, including the British Isles, was engulfed in often violent conflict between Protestants and Catholics. The Church of England, although not as zealously Protestant as many of the other religious sects in England and Scotland, had broken from the Roman Catholic Church in 1534, and brutality toward Irish Catholics characterized English rule in Ireland. Richard accepted only Irish Protestants as tenants and ran Catholics off his lands.

Richard's good fortune gave him a strong sense that God was intervening on his behalf. "God's Province is my inheritance," he once wrote. Robert, although he would have likely put it in humbler terms, inherited this same conviction that God was looking out for him.

The earl also believed in education and provided his children—even his daughters—with books and tutors. When Robert was eight years old, he and his brother Francis were sent across the Irish Channel to attend a British boarding school named Eton College. Francis, two years older, was friendly, outgoing, and sportive. Robert was quieter and often could be found in a corner with a book. The boys were also accompanied by a personal tutor named Mr. Carew, who wrote to the earl that Robert "prefers learning above all other virtues or pleasures."

Eton, which was established in the 1400s, was considered to be the best secondary school in England. The boys attended classes and church services and were also encouraged to play games such as cricket, rugby, and rowing.

Eton College, located about one mile north of Windsor Castle and approximately thirty miles from London, was founded in 1440 by King Henry VI. Boyle attended the school from 1635 to 1638. (Courtesy of the Granger Collection.)

Robert made excuses to stay out of sports and hid away in his rooms to read during morning recess. His studies included Latin, mathematics, history, logic, and Bible study, and he was frequently exposed to the ancient writings of Aristotle, Hippocrates, Galen, and other classical thinkers.

The ancient Greek philosopher Aristotle was the most important figure in science, which was called Natural Philosophy in the sixteenth century, or the study of the natural world, before the sixteenth century. In his writings on science Aristotle had divided the universe into two spheres: the sublunary region, from the Earth to the Moon, and an outer sphere reaching from the Moon to a fixed curtain of stars.

The universe was finite in Aristotle's system, and the outer sphere, which was composed of only one element, ether, never changed. Conversely, the sublunary sphere, composed of four intermingled elements—earth, air, fire, and water—was in constant flux. Aristotle believed the ongoing changes in the sublunary sphere occurred because each of the four elements had an inherent drive to separate from the others. Earth, for example, was the heaviest of the elements, which explained why the planet was in the

This fifteenth-century drawing depicts an Aristotelian interpretation of the four elements, with earth, the heaviest, at the bottom. (Courtesy of the Granger Collection.)

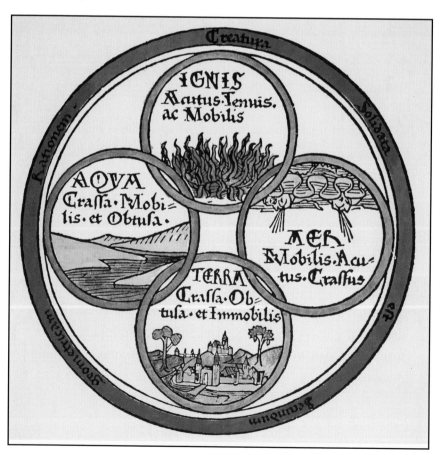

center of the universe. Fire and air, the lightest elements, were ceaselessly attempting to escape upward; water was the second heaviest and drawn to earth.

The ideas of Aristotle and other ancient thinkers had been reintroduced into Western Europe in the twelfth century and quickly gained acceptance in the universities and among intellectuals. An academic school of thought known as Scholasticism was developed to reconcile Aristotle's teachings with Christian theology. Because it was said Aristotle had walked while delivering his lectures, his followers in the European universities came to be known as Peripatetics, which means "walking."

Much of the work done during what we today call the Scientific Revolution—particularly in the early years—inevitably challenged Aristotle. The fundamental difference was in how thinkers reached conclusions. Modern science relies on observation, experimentation, and quantitative evaluation. Aristotle rejected the use of experimentation and the idea that mathematical analysis could both describe and reveal nature.

When Boyle went to Eton to study, challenges to Aristotle's system had already been developed and were gaining credence. The provost of Eton, Sir Henry Wotton, was interested in natural philosophy and was a critic of the Peripatetics. He often invited the most promising of the students, including Robert, to his house to dine and discuss academic topics. (At one of Robert's visits to Wotton's house, he met the English poet and theologian John Milton, the author of *Paradise Lost*.) Wotton let the students explore his small chemical laboratory and described to them what was known as the "Baconian Method," after the English philosopher and essayist Francis Bacon.

Bacon, who happened to be a cousin of Wotton's, was an early opponent of the Peripatetics' idea that knowledge should be arrived at through pure logic and deduction— a view that even Aristotle had not held as tightly as his Peripatetic disciples often did. Bacon thought that as "natural philosophers," scientists should learn inductively, through study, observation, and experiment. He urged the students to free their minds of prejudices and preconceived ideas, which he called "idols." Bacon was not much of an experimentalist himself, however. In his most famous experiment, he ran out into the cold on a freezing day and stuffed a chicken full of snow to see whether the cold would preserve it. He contracted pneumonia as a result of the experiment and died at the age of sixty-five.

Bacon was not the only one to have questioned the teachings of Aristotle. Wotton also introduced Robert to the scientific writings of Nicolas Copernicus, Galileo Galilei, and Johannes Kepler, all of whom, along with other Renaissance scholars, had begun the process of developing the modern scientific method.

Robert also read William Harvey's *On the Motion of the Blood* and discussed it with Wotton. Harvey had discovered that the heart could pump seven gallons of blood every hour, but his results contradicted the writings of Galen, an ancient Greek who said the liver constantly made new blood that was pumped to various parts of the body. Harvey realized it was impossible for the liver to make that much new blood, so he continued experimenting until he proved that the liver was not involved in pumping blood at all; instead, arteries carry blood away from the heart and veins carry blood toward the heart. Robert was intrigued by how much Harvey had learned by experiments and observation.

Eton's headmaster, John Harrison, also took young Robert under his wing. Harrison allowed Robert extended holidays and excused him from some of his classes so he could privately tutor him. Robert later wrote that he used his free time "so greedily in reading, that [my] master would sometimes be necessitated to force [me] out to play." Robert's voracious reading often left him distracted. Once, after reading a book of romantic tales, he was so affected by it that he had to solve complex algebraic equations in his head to bring his mind back into focus, or "to fetter, or at least to curb the roving wildness of [my] wandering thoughts."

Robert was often sick during his time at Eton. Fevers and stomach problems plagued him, but there was little he could do. Once, when he had trouble shaking off a fever, a doctor sent him a new medicine. When he took it, Robert felt as if his stomach was going to explode and he was violently sick and weak for days. The doctor had given him the wrong medicine. For the rest of his life, Robert viewed doctors skeptically, although he was a personal friend to several. He would often mix his own medicines and potions in his laboratory.

Robert lived in the two-hundred-year-old home of his headmaster and tutor, John Harrison. One evening, while Robert was in bed and his brother Francis talked with three friends, a whole section of the house wall suddenly gave way. Bricks and dust fell down upon the boys, but luckily they were not seriously injured. Robert saw his own survival as an act of divine providence, which reinforced his faith as a devout Anglican.

At the end of 1638, both Sir Henry Wotton and John Harrison left Eton. The school's new headmaster was a rigid disciplinarian, and Robert began to lose interest in his studies. His father decided it was time for his sons to return home. The years that Robert spent at Eton were the only formal schooling he received. From then on, he relied exclusively on tutors and on his own reading and experimentation.

While Robert and Francis had been off at school, their father had fallen on hard times. In 1633, a man named Thomas Wentworth was appointed as the Lord Deputy of Ireland, a position that Richard had wanted for himself. Wentworth saw the powerful Earl of Cork as a threat and set out to ruin him. He levied several high taxes on Richard and involved him in a costly lawsuit, eventually extracting the exorbitant sum of 15,000 pounds from the earl. In 1638, at the age of seventy-two, Richard left Ireland for a new estate in Stalbridge, England, an all-but-defeated man.

After a brief stay with their father at Stalbridge, Robert and Francis prepared to embark on a tour of continental Europe with their new tutor, a Huguenot (a French Protestant) named Isaac Marcombes. The trip was one of the most formative experiences in young Robert's life. Before they left, however, the earl hastily arranged a marriage for Francis with Elizabeth Killigrew, the daughter of one of Richard's wealthy friends. The earl intended to hold the wedding after the boys had returned from Europe, but King Charles I insisted that they do it immediately. King Charles—who, incidentally, spoke with a slight stammer similar to Robert's—attended the wedding, gave away the bride, and then saw the new couple off to bed. Elizabeth would later become a mistress of King Charles's son, Charles II; she would be known as "Black Betty" and bear the king an illegitimate son.

Soon after the wedding, twelve-year-old Robert and sixteen-year-old Francis set off with Marcombes on their grand tour. They traveled through France on horseback, visited Paris, and then proceeded to Geneva, Switzerland, where Marcombes had a wife and family. Throughout the winter, Robert and Francis stayed at their tutor's home and studied under him. Marcombes, a practical, demanding teacher, taught Robert and Francis in a number of disciplines, including Latin, logic, rhetoric, history, the Bible, and geography. Both learned to speak French well enough to pass as Frenchmen. Robert also excelled at mathematics and continued his interest in science.

Robert's time in Geneva was also religiously formative, and despite his scientific inclination, he tended to look for divine messages in natural events. One night, as a terrifying thunderstorm pounded Geneva, thirteen-year-old Robert

> was suddenly waked in a fright with such loud claps
> of thunder . . . and every clap was both preceded and
> attended with flashes of lightning so numerous and
> so dazzling that [I] began to imagine them the sallies
> of fire that must consume the world.

Robert felt that Judgment Day was at hand:

> Whereupon the consideration of [my] unpreparedness
> to welcome it, and the hideousness of being surprised
> by it in an unfit condition, made [me] resolve and
> vow, that if [my] fears were that night disappointed,
> all [my] future additions to [my] life should be more
> religiously and watchfully employed.

After the harrowing storm, he vowed to be more faithful to God. But he also worried that his faith was based more on a fear of damnation than on true piety. A short time later, after visiting an abbey in the mountains, Robert was overcome by a "deep raving melancholy" and even briefly contemplated suicide. He came to see it as his goal to overcome these doubts so he could live a devout life.

After living in Geneva for two years, Robert and Francis began to grow restless and longed to see more of Europe. They pressed their father to let them travel to Italy, but Richard worried they would be converted to Catholicism. He also feared for their safety. Tension between Catholic Italy and Protestant England was at a fever pitch, especially since a London mob had killed an Italian priest. But Richard finally relented: The boys could go to Italy, but only if they pretended to be Frenchmen, whom Italians tended to receive more hospitably than Englishmen. After journeying through the Alps and into Italy, Robert, Francis, and Marcombes visited Venice, Verona, Padua, Florence, and Rome. They saw famous buildings and beautiful works of art. But Robert had a special request—he wanted to meet Galileo Galilei.

Galileo, whose writings Robert had first read at Eton on Wotton's advice, is sometimes called the father of modern science. He made important astronomical observations, which he wrote about in a popular book called *The Starry Messenger* and performed experiments on acceleration and motion. Galileo shared Francis Bacon's view that natural philosophy should be separated from religion and that all conclusions should be based on observations and experiments.

Another one of Galileo's books, *Dialogue Concerning the Two Chief Systems of the World,* supported the theory originally put forth by Nicolas Copernicus in his 1543 work *On the Revolutions of Heavenly Spheres* that the earth rotates around the sun. Galileo's book ran counter to Church doctrine and in 1633 Galileo was placed under house arrest at his villa outside Florence, where he was living at the time Robert and Francis visited. Unfortunately, Galileo died before Robert could meet him.

After Galileo died, Robert took a renewed interest in his work. His reading of Galileo may have inspired him to focus on science, although he maintained interest in other

Astronomer, mathematician, and physicist Galileo under house arrest in the 1630s after being condemned by the holy court of the Catholic Church in Rome. (Courtesy of the Granger Collection.)

intellectual pursuits. Robert thought the Catholic Church's persecution of Galileo was a travesty.

By inclination and upbringing, Robert shared with many of his Protestant contemporaries a strong distaste for Roman Catholicism that his experience in Italy only confirmed. Marcombes took Robert and Francis for a tour of the famous Florentine Bordellos, or brothels, in an effort to show them the excesses of Catholic Italy. Robert was repulsed by the spectacle. His antipathy toward Catholicism was lifelong.

As the brothers and their tutor resumed their travels through Europe, trouble was brewing in Ireland. Although Richard had been a fair landlord by the standards of the day, other Englishmen had ruled as tyrants over their Irish subjects and many Irish Catholics objected to Protestant rule. A rebellion broke out in 1641, and Richard was forced to return to defend his estates. The rebellion would eventually drain the family's coffers and kill two of Robert's brothers.

When Robert and Francis arrived in Marseilles, France, they received a message from their father to hurry home to Ireland. The message was sent with money for their travel, but a messenger stole it en route. The brothers managed to scrape together enough money for Francis to return, but Robert, who had fallen ill, returned to Geneva and lived with his tutor for two more years while his father and brothers fought the rebels.

Ireland was not the only place where there was unrest. England was entering a civil war that would rage for the next ten years. The war pitted the supporters of King Charles, or Royalists, against the Parliamentarians, also known as "Roundheads" for the closely cropped hairstyle they wore. The causes of the English Civil War were complex, but in large part it was a religious conflict. Many English Puritans and Presbyterians, especially in Scotland, objected to what they regarded as "papist," or Catholic, influence in England. When the Anglican Church had broken away, it had retained a number of liturgical rites reminiscent of Catholic services, such as the use of altars and a communion service. King Charles had also married a Catholic, the French princess Henrietta Maria.

The English Civil War was also a political struggle between Parliament and the king. In the past, the monarch had used Parliament to raise extra taxes when he or she needed to and had assumed the power to dissolve Parliament at any time. Wiser rulers, such as Elizabeth I, had usually been careful not to abuse the power, but King Charles I insisted his power was absolute. He dissolved a parliament in 1626 and did not call another into session for eleven years. This angered many noblemen who began to question the king's belief in his absolute authority. When Charles was forced to reconvene Parliament in 1640 it would come to be known as the "Long Parliament" because it refused the king's order to dissolve and sat continuously for thirteen years. Charles called on Parliament to raise money to pay for troops to put down rebellions in Scotland and Ireland, but he refused to honor Parliament's demand that he accept limits on his power. In 1642 both sides raised armies, and civil war broke out.

The Parliamentarians held London from the beginning;

the king moved his court to Oxford. Besieged at home and stretched thin, Charles signed a treaty ending the Irish conflict. As part of the treaty, Robert's father had to give up Lismore Castle, where Robert had been born. The treaty was a heavy blow to Richard Boyle and he never recovered. Nearly penniless and broken-hearted, he died in September 1643.

dilettante

scientist

In 1644, seventeen-year-old Robert Boyle returned to England after living abroad for five years. However, the war had scattered his family members, and young Robert did not know where to find them. For a time, he cast about London and even considered joining the Royalist army. Then, by sheer coincidence, he ran into his older sister Katherine while walking along a London street. At first, she did not recognize him because of his French clothes, but when he spoke, "she cried out, 'Oh! 'Tis my brother,' with the joy and tenderness of a most affectionate sister," as Robert later recounted. Katherine invited Robert to live with her and her children.

Katherine was twelve years older than Robert, but she had always been close to him and had cared for him after their mother died. She was intelligent, lively, and independent.

Boyle's sister Katherine, known as Lady Ranelagh. (British Library)

A friend wrote of her that she was "one of the most beautiful as well as the most talented of her time." She had a phenomenal memory and could hear a sermon in church and write it out verbatim when she returned home. As with most of the Earl of Cork's children, Katherine was married off at a young age. Her husband, Lord Ranelagh, was an abusive Anglo-Irish nobleman who fortunately spent most of his time in Ireland while she was allowed to stay in England. Katherine was known as Lady Ranelagh.

Before he died, Richard Boyle had arranged a marriage between Robert and a nobleman's daughter named Lady Ann Howard. On Boyle's return from Europe, his sister told him that when Lady Howard's father had heard of the Boyle family's misfortunes, he had married her to another man. Boyle would never marry, although his wealth, good manners, and attractive if peculiar looks made him a desirable mate.

Katherine also informed Robert that, because of his father's death, he was the heir to the earl's manor at Stalbridge, in County Dorset. Boyle was not sure if his title to Stalbridge would be secure—his father had been a staunch Royalist, and Stalbridge fell in and out of the control of Parliamentary forces. Katherine, however, had Parliamentarian sympathies and connections and used her influence to keep the estate safe.

After briefly returning to France to repay Marcombes for funding his extended stay in Europe, Boyle proceeded to Stalbridge, where he found the estate in almost complete disrepair. The house was deteriorating, the fields were full of weeds, and one of his father's former servants had embezzled a great deal of money. Boyle fired the man and set to work fixing everything.

Once his estate was in order, Boyle settled into a quiet, solitary life of study and reflection. He read voluminously,

Boyle conducted many of his experiments at Stalbridge House during his residence there from 1644 through 1655. (British Library)

and wrote on a number of subjects, including philosophy and religion. He lived at Stalbridge for the next ten years.

Although Boyle had earlier shown an interest in natural philosophy, he began his studies in earnest at Stalbridge. The field of chemistry, in which most of Boyle's most famous work was done, did not yet exist. Most people who did what we would today call chemistry called themselves "alchemists." Alchemy was a medieval mixture of chemical experimentation and speculative, mystical philosophy that aimed to transform common metals into gold. Alchemy also sought to discover a panacea, or universal cure for disease, as well as a way to prolong life.

Over the previous five hundred years, from the twelfth century on, Europe had been the center of alchemical research. Because of a constant fear among devotees that others might uncover their secrets, practitioners wrote mostly in secret codes. Instructions for alchemical procedures were usually couched in mystical, cryptic language, in part to keep the uninitiated from having access to the experiments. The alchemists' motto was "Never reveal clearly to anyone any discovery, but be sufficient unto thyself." Many of the goals of alchemy were predicated on Aristotle's theory of the four elements. Because, according to Aristotle, everything in the sublunary sphere consisted of fire, earth, air, and water, and the elements were in a constant state of flux, alchemists deduced it should be possible to find a way to physically change materials through a process called transmutation.

Though its exact origins are not known, alchemy was practiced in ancient China, Egypt, and India, often in conjunction with astrology, as well as in Europe. The alchemist's ultimate goal was to discover the so-called philosopher's stone, which could be used to transform metals. It was said the elixir could also transform people and make them immortal or give them other magical powers.

Not all the efforts of the alchemists were wasted. While looking for gold and panaceas, alchemists invented and improved all types of equipment and methods, eventually forming the basis for modern chemistry. Their methods were used to refine metal from ores, make medicines, and perfect a number of metalworking and glass-making techniques. Most importantly, they put a heavy emphasis on experimentation, although not always in a systematic way. Boyle performed numerous alchemical experiments in his laboratory and worked to decipher the codes used by other alchemists.

Boyle's first efforts at alchemy were not very fruitful. He ordered glassware, crucibles, chemicals, and other equipment from local artisans, but he needed a special kind of furnace to provide heat for his experiments. On the advice of Marcombes, he ordered one from Holland, where they used the furnaces to glaze china. Impatiently waiting for his furnace to arrive at Stalbridge, Boyle wrote to Katherine that he believed it was being transported on a wagon pulled by snails. When it finally arrived, it was broken, "into as many pieces as we into sects." He was alluding to the violence and religious sectarianism of the English Civil War. "I have been so unlucky in my first attempts at chemistry," he also wrote. He decided to travel to Holland and bring a furnace back himself.

When he had finally set up his laboratory, Boyle began experiments with fire and metals and practiced distillations—a method of boiling and then cooling a substance to make it purer—with various liquids. He enjoyed experimenting with his new furnace. "Vulcan [the Roman god of fire] has so transported and bewitched me that as the delights I taste in it make me fancy my laboratory a kind of Elysium [paradise]," he wrote to Katherine. He recorded the procedures and results of his experiments in notebooks.

Boyle's alchemical experiments might have been somewhat hampered because he had doubts about Aristotle's theory of the four elements. Nature was too diverse; it seemed to him there had to be more than four elements. He did believe in transmutation, however, and many of his experiments at Stalbridge were attempts to change one substance into another. He never succeeded but learned about the process of chemical experimentation in the process.

During his time at Stalbridge, Boyle also wrote several nature essays that he sent to his sister. Years later, when Boyle was famous as a scientist, she convinced him to publish the essays in a book called *Occasional Reflections*. The recurring theme in the essays was the significance of seemingly mundane objects and experiences. The book was widely read and influenced the genre of the short essay.

In one essay, "Reflection Upon the Eating of Oysters," Boyle describes two friends enjoying a meal of oysters. One friend reflects that, to foreigners with different customs, the practice of eating raw oysters may seem as barbarous as eating raw meat. The other friend responds with the idea of a short story, describing "an observing native" from "some island of the southern ocean, governed by such rational laws and customs, as those in *Utopia*, or the *New Atlantis*," who:

> upon his return home from his travels made in Europe, should give an account of our countries and manners, under feigned names, and frequently intimate in his relations, (or in his answers to questions that should be made him) the reasons of his wondering to find

A contemporary of Boyle, the Anglo-Irish writer Jonathan Swift was a well-known satirist, essayist, and clergyman. (Courtesy of the Granger Collection.)

our customs so extravagant, and differing from those of his country.

"Reflection Upon the Eating of Oysters" was rumored to have inspired Jonathan Swift to write his masterpiece, *Gulliver's Travels*.

Boyle certainly did provoke Swift to write another satire, "A Meditation upon a Broom-Stick," which mocked the wistful, somewhat pompous tone of *Occasional Reflections*.

The poet Samuel Butler also satirized Boyle's book in an essay called "An Occasional Reflection on Dr. Charlton's Feeling a Dog's Pulse at Gresham College."

Boyle also wrote religious tracts that were, as a rule, very pious and moralistic, such as the long essay "A Free Discourse against Customary Swearing." There was also a novel called *The Martyrdom of Theodora and Diymus,* written in a similar vein. Boyle never felt that his commitment to science undermined his religious faith. He always gave a reverent pause before saying the name of God.

In seventeenth-century London, coffeehouses often functioned as meeting places for intellectuals, such as the members of the Invisible College, to discuss their work, theories, and ideas. (Courtesy of Art Resource.)

Although Boyle spent most of his time at Stalbridge alone, he occasionally traveled to London to stay with his sister. Lady Ranelagh's home was a meeting place for a number of prominent London intellectuals. Boyle enjoyed their company, and they soon formed a group that came to be called the "Invisible College." In addition to meeting at Lady Ranelagh's house, they also congregated in taverns, coffeehouses, and at Gresham College in London. Members included the astronomer and architect Christopher Wren, the clergyman John Wilkins, and the physician Jonathan Goddard.

These men practiced the experimental philosophy proposed by Francis Bacon and other natural philosophers, which came to be known as the "New Philosophy." In their view, questions about the natural world could only be answered by experimentation. They also believed in the free exchange of ideas and information. Boyle's friend Samuel Hartlib took the lead in establishing a communication network through letters in which they shared information and the results of individual experiments. When Boyle could not travel to London to meet with the Invisible College, he kept in touch through letters.

While Boyle enjoyed relative quiet at his manor in Dorset, the rest of the country was immersed in civil strife. In 1649, King Charles I was beheaded by Parliamentarian forces, which were now being led by a Puritan general named Oliver Cromwell. After Charles's execution, the so-called Rump Parliament—the remnant of the Long Parliament left after its Royalists members were purged—abolished the monarchy and established the Commonwealth of England. Charles I's son, who would later reign as Charles II, fled in exile to France and then to Holland.

Although Boyle harbored Royalist sympathies, he tried to stay above the fray, and was angered and saddened by the violence. The Anglican Church had been the supreme authority in England, now the country was divided. Minor differences in liturgical rites provoked fierce debate and violence. Boyle wrote:

> It has been long, as well my wonder, as my grief, to see such comparatively petty differences in judgement make such wide breaches and vast divisions in affection. It is strange, that men should rather be quarrelling for a few trifling opinions, wherein they dissent, than to embrace one another for those many fundamental truths, wherein they agree.

As different factions and religious sects vied for power and influence in the new government, Boyle feared that Stalbridge was in danger again, but he need not have worried. Robert's brothers had spent the last several years successfully fighting off the rebels in Ireland. Whoever ruled England could not afford to have another Irish rebellion on their hands, which kept the Boyle family safe from interference.

When the fighting finally died down, Boyle traveled to Ireland to inspect and tend to the family property there. He spent two unhappy years in Ireland, during which time he had very limited contact with members of the Invisible

College. He did, however, have the opportunity to study with a physician named William Petty, who taught Boyle anatomy and physiology through performing dissections and examining specimens under microscopes. Boyle wrote that in Ireland he had seen "more of the variety and contrivances of nature, and the majesty and wisdom of her author, than in all the books I ever read in my life could give me convincing notions of."

Languishing in Ireland, Boyle longed to be back amid the stimulation of his intellectual peers. Fortunately, now that his Irish estates were in order, Boyle was once again a rich man. The rents brought in an income of 3,000 pounds a year. He could afford to devote his time to experiments and have money to buy equipment and supplies. He decided to leave his estate in England the care of his brother Francis, who already held estates in the adjoining area.

Boyle briefly considered moving to London, but the turmoil of the war had driven various members of the Invisible College, many of whom had Royalist sympathies, to Oxford. Boyle's friend John Wilkins, who was the warden of Wadham College, encouraged Robert to join them. Boyle rented an apartment and set up his laboratory at a house on High Street in Oxford.

Boyle's time at Stalbridge, and with Petty in Ireland, had given him a solid grounding in alchemy and scientific methods, but he was still a dilettante. Although he took his studies seriously, science was only one of his many interests.

THREE

the spring of air

When Boyle arrived at Oxford in 1654, the university's chancellor was none other than Oliver Cromwell, the most powerful man in England. After orchestrating the king's execution, Cromwell had quashed the remaining Royalist resistance in Ireland and Scotland, had dissolved the Rump Parliament, and ruled the country alone. He took on the chancellorship of Oxford in addition to his other duties because he wanted to seize the once-Royalist institution and use it to instill Puritan values into the country's educated elite.

Under Cromwell's leadership, Oxford's enrollment and funding swelled, and the university became the foremost center of learning in England. Wadham College, in particular, led by Boyle's friend John Wilkins, became a home

Oxford's main road, High Street, cuts prominently through the center of town.
(Library of Congress)

for theologians and natural philosophers interested in the New Philosophy.

Boyle wanted to be brought up to speed with current scientific thinking. He hired a German chemist named Peter Stahl as a tutor and spent his first six years in Oxford immersed in learning about science, building up his laboratory, and dabbling in new experiments.

On the recommendation of his friend Dr. Thomas Willis, Boyle also hired an Oxford student named Robert Hooke as his laboratory assistant. Hooke was a mechanical genius who, during his distinguished career, would improve on the designs of telescopes, microscopes, thermometers, and barometers. Many of Hooke's contemporaries, including Sir Isaac Newton, with whom Hooke would later share a bitter rivalry, found him to be abrasive and confrontational, but Hooke and Boyle enjoyed a warm friendship. They also collaborated to make some of the most important observations and discoveries ever made on the properties of air.

At the time Boyle began experimenting on air, several significant, false assumptions about the nature of matter continued to loom large. Aristotle had proposed that all matter is continuous and had rejected the idea of a vacuum—a space devoid of matter—as impossible. Because the world was finite and filled with the four elements in a continuous flux, any potential void was instantly filled. Furthermore, because he assumed that speed was proportional to force, Aristotle reasoned that a finite force in a vacuum would produce an infinite speed because a vacuum would be frictionless. The idea that a vacuum was impossible had led thinkers and theologians who followed Aristotle to develop a concept called *horror vacui*, or "nature abhors a vacuum."

The Frenchman René Descartes, one of the most important and influential natural philosophers of the seventeenth century, also rejected the idea of a vacuum. Descartes rejected the idea of vacuums because it did not fit into his overarching explanation of how the universe operated. In Descartes' cosmic system, all matter in the universe was connected by invisible, but material, vortices that were supported by an invisible fluid similar to Aristotle's ether. All motions were controlled by these vortices, from the motion of the planets around the sun to the smallest motions on Earth.

It might seem surprising that Descartes, a respected mathematician, would propose that the planets were motivated and supported in their orbits by an invisible, material fluid. Descartes was a Catholic and may have been partly influenced by the trial of Galileo and wanted to escape a similar imprisonment. However, there are other reasons why he would not accept the possible existence of voids. If he accepted the possibility of a vacuum, it suddenly became necessary to explain how gravity operated without a physical connection between the planets and the sun. It was not until later in the century that Isaac Newton would mathematically explain that gravity worked by attraction, not propulsion, without a material connection.

Another Aristotelian tenet was that air was weightless, but this was also being called into question. In 1643, a former assistant of Galileo's named Evangelista Torricelli began conducting a series of experiments to determine if air did have pressure, which would be impossible if air was weightless. In his most famous experiment, Torricelli sealed one end of a glass tube and immersed the open end in a bowl of mercury. The mercury was forced up into the tube at a level much higher than the level of mercury in the bowl. Torrecelli determined that the force lifting the mercury into the tube was atmospheric pressure. He repeated the experiment several times and found that the same amount of mercury stayed in the tube.

Torricelli decided that the weight of the mercury column

in the tube was equal to the weight of the air column pushing down on the bowl of mercury. He also reasoned that the greater the air pressure, the higher the mercury would rise in the tube, and at lower pressure the mercury level would drop. Clearly, air had weight, and it could be measured by determining the level of mercury in the tube.

This nineteenth-century engraving depicts Evangelista Torricelli in the process of inventing the barometer. (Courtesy of the Granger Collection.)

Torricelli also noticed that the height of the mercury column varied, depending on weather conditions. The atmosphere "is sometimes heavier and denser and at other times lighter and thinner," Torricelli wrote, and it could be detected by the changing mercury level in the tube. He had invented the barometer, the instrument Boyle would later use to predict the storm of 1658.

Even though he did not know it, Torricelli had also created a vacuum: the unfilled space in top of the tube. When he died in 1647, others carried on his work. A French scientist and mathematician named Blaise Pascal wondered what a barometer would do at a high altitude. As he was too ill to perform the experiment himself, Pascal convinced his brother-in-law to measure the height of a barometer at the bottom of a mountain and then take the same measurements one mile higher. The difference was three inches of mercury, ten percent of the total.

The invention of the barometer was not the only new technology developed in this period. In 1654, the same year Boyle came to Oxford, a German scientist named Otto von Guericke built an air pump by fitting together two copper hemispheres into a globe. On one side of the globe von Guericke attached a valve to an air pump that allowed him to pump all of the air from the sphere. After pumping out the air, he had ropes attached to the sphere's sides. He then hitched teams of eight horses on each side of the globe to try to pull it apart, but it would not separate. But, when the valve was opened and air rushed back in, the globe fell apart on its own.

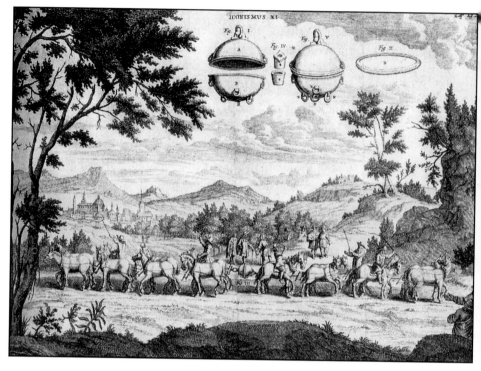

Otto von Guericke's 1654 experiment in Magdeburg, Germany, in which sixteen horses failed to separate the two halves of his globe. (From Guericke's *Experimenta Nova*)

When the air had been pumped out, a vacuum had been created in the globe.

Other scientists suggested that the vacuum inside the globe was what held it together, but von Guericke thought that it was the force of the air, the atmosphere, operating on the outside. When air was pumped back into the globe, the air pressure inside was equal to the air pressure on the outside, and the pieces separated.

When Boyle read about von Guericke's air pump, he was intrigued and decided to build one of his own. Von

Guericke's sphere was made of copper, but Boyle wanted his to be a glass ball so he could observe what happened to items placed inside the vacuum. When an instrument maker in London could not make a pump to Boyle's specifications, he had Hooke build it.

Boyle's pump pulled air out of the glass chamber, producing a vacuum. Brass pipes connected the pump's pistons and cylinders to the glass globe, and leather valves allowed air to pass only one way. The glass chamber had a hole at the top so objects could be placed inside and had a stopper to keep air out during experiments. The bell-shaped chamber was large enough to hold two fairly large items. Von Guericke's pump had required two strong men to operate, but one man could easily operate Hooke's model.

In one of his first experiments with the air pump, Boyle half-filled a sheep's bladder with air, tied it off with a string, and placed it inside the chamber. As air was pumped out of the chamber, the sheep's bladder swelled until it was close to bursting. Boyle wrote in his notebook, "the bladder appeared as full and stretched as if it had been blown up." When air was returned to the chamber, the bladder deflated. Boyle guessed that the air in the bladder expanded as the air in the chamber was forced out or, as he wrote, "the bladder was proportionally compressed."

This first experiment whetted Boyle's curiosity. He made long lists of experiments to try with the air pump. Would a candle burn inside the vacuum? What would happen to a small living thing such as a bird? What about magnets, watches?

Boyle continued to experiment with the air pump and recorded his findings in notebooks and reported on them to the Invisible College. While most earlier experimenters had only recorded successful experiments, Boyle recorded both successes and failures. He even published a pamphlet called *Of Unsucceeding Experiments* that pointed out the value of failed experiments to advance learning and understanding.

In one experiment Boyle lowered a lit candle into the glass chamber and put the stopper in the hole. The candle went out after about five minutes. Next, he re-lit the candle, put it back in the chamber, and began pumping out air, and the candle went out in less than a minute. He also observed that smoke rose to the top of the chamber when air was present, but fell to the bottom in a vacuum. A hot coal placed in the chamber would go out when the air was evacuated, but if the coal was still hot when air was let back in, the coal would light up again. Boyle concluded that there was something in the air that was necessary to keep both the candle and the coal burning.

Boyle numbered his experiments. For experiment sixteen, he placed a compass in the glass globe and held a magnet to the side of the glass. As expected, the compass needle moved toward the magnet. When air was pumped out with the compass still in the chamber, the compass again moved toward the magnet. Apparently, magnetism still worked in a vacuum.

A ticking watch yielded another interesting result. Hooke removed the cover of his pocket watch so that he

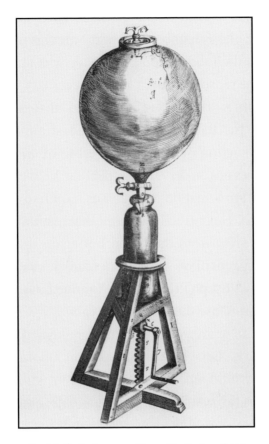

Boyle's first air pump. (From *The Spring of Air*)

and Boyle could see its inner machinery move and put the watch into the glass chamber. As the air was pumped out, the ticking sounds grew softer and softer until they could no longer hear it. The gears still turned, which meant it was ticking, but in the vacuum it made no sound. When air was slowly let back into the chamber, the ticking grew louder and louder. Boyle deduced that sound does not travel in a vacuum.

Boyle also placed small animals, such as mice and birds, in the glass chamber. When the air was pumped out, the animals died. Something in the air was necessary for breathing, he reasoned, just as it was necessary for a candle to stay burning. "For we see," he wrote, "that in our engine [the pump] the flame of a lamp will last almost as little after the exsuction of the air, as the life of an animal."

Boyle did not make the connection between burning and respiration—that both processes require oxygen—but he was close. He correctly thought that respiration carried off toxic wastes from the blood but again did not know the role oxygen plays in the circulatory system. In the next century, Joseph Priestly and Antoine Lavoisier would discover and name the element oxygen.

Boyle's air pump soon became a regular fixture when the Invisible College held meetings at his laboratory. Boyle and Hooke would repeat their experiments with the animal bladder, candle, watch, compass, animals, and magnet in front of admiring audiences of other scientists. One of Boyle's colleagues composed an amusing poem about the experimental work of the group, which includes the following lines about Boyle's experiments with the air pump:

To the Danish Agent late was showne
That where noe Ayre is, there's no breath.
A glasse this secret did make knowne
Wherein a Catt was put to death.
Out of the glasse the Ayre being screwed,
Puss dyed and ne'er so much as mewed.

The self same glasse did likewise clear
Another secret more profound:
That nought but Ayre unto the Eare
Can be the Medium of Sound
For in the glasse emptied of Ayre
A striking watch you cannot hear.

When word of Blaise Pascal's experiment—the one
in which his brother-in-law brought a barometer up a
mountain—filtered into the scientific community at Oxford, Boyle was dismayed to find out the news was ten
years old. Clearly, a better method of spreading scientific
knowledge was needed. Boyle's friends Henry Oldenburg
and Samuel Hartlib set up a faster system to disseminate
information. They began receiving letters from scientists
all over Europe reporting on their work. They would then
send the information on to others. Oldenburg also wrote
clear copies of various scientists' work and published it.
The more scientists knew of other scientists' successes
and failures, the more they could all learn. Boyle kept up
with the work others were doing and continued to keep
detailed notebooks.

Boyle placed a barometer in the glass chamber of his air
pump. As his assistants pumped the air out, Boyle watched
the mercury level in the barometer drop. The assistants
pumped and pumped, but they could not get the mercury
to fall lower than half an inch.

Boyle speculated that his air pump could not form a
complete vacuum, which meant Torricelli had been right
when he said the mercury column was reacting to air

pressure. It was not the "suction" caused by the vacuum that made it rise in the tube. Today it is known that, physically speaking, there is no such thing as suction. When someone drinks from a straw, for example, a vacuum is created in both the mouth and the straw, which lowers the air pressure relative to the pressure pushing on the surface of the fluid in the cup, forcing the liquid up through the straw and into the mouth.

Putting the barometer in the air pump yielded the same result as taking it up a mountain. When air was let into the chamber, the column rose. Now convinced the barometer could predict the weather, Boyle and Hooke began to record the barometer reading every morning and evening.

Boyle, who had always had a strong affinity for Galileo, decided to use his air pump to perform an experiment Galileo had proposed years before. Galileo had stated that without air resistance all objects would fall at the same rate, regardless of their weight. This seemed counterintuitive and contrary to experience—a heavy piece of lead certainly falls faster than a feather. Galileo said this was due to air resistance. If dropped in a vacuum, he insisted, both would hit the ground at the same time. Galileo tried to demonstrate this principle by rolling two balls of different sizes and weights down a ramp, but because he had no way of producing a vacuum, he could never fully test his theory.

Boyle took up the challenge. He attached a long glass tube to his air pump and rested a feather and a piece of lead inside it. After the air pump had evacuated the air inside both the chamber and the tube, Boyle flipped the tube upside down and watched the feather and lead fall. Both hit the bottom of the tube at the same time; Galileo had been right. Boyle later held up the experiment as a demonstration of why "we assent to experience, even when its information seems contrary to reason."

As Boyle toiled away in his private laboratory in Oxford, England fell even more completely into the hands of Oliver Cromwell. During his five years in power, Cromwell ruled with an imperious hand. In 1657 a reconstituted parliament

Painted in 1649 by Robert Walker, this portrait of Oliver Cromwell was made before he became Lord Protector. (Courtesy of the Granger Collection.)

even offered him the crown, but Cromwell declined the honor. Instead, he installed himself as "Lord Protector," with even more expansive powers than he had enjoyed before. A year later, however, Cromwell died, three days after the legendary storm Boyle had predicted with his barometer.

Interestingly, during the same terrible storm of 1658 another famous scientist, only sixteen years old at the time, performed what he later claimed was his first experiment. Isaac Newton, then attending school in a town named Grantham, wanted to measure the force of the wind. He went out into the storm and first jumped into the air with the wind, and then against the wind, and marked how much the wind impeded or enabled his movement.

Sometime before 1657, Boyle met the famous physician William Harvey, whose work on the circulation of blood he had read about as a student. When Boyle asked Harvey what had given him the idea that blood circulated, Harvey said he had realized as he studied the body's veins, arteries, and valves that "nature had not so placed so many valves without design; and no design seemed more probable than—that the blood should be sent through the arteries, and return through the veins, whose valves did not oppose its course that way." This type of thinking—the belief that God's design was evident in nature—also characterized Boyle's thinking and the thinking of many natural philosophers in the seventeenth and eighteenth centuries.

Boyle was not finished experimenting with the atmosphere. He and his assistants constructed a thirty-two-foot-long tin pipe and connected it at the top to a three-foot-long glass tube. They then moved the air pump to the roof of a four-story building, attached it to the pipes, and placed the bottom of the pipe in a tub of water on ground level. With all of his assistants working the air pump, they were able to raise the water to a height of thirty-three feet six inches. Without the air pump, the water level had not risen because the air pressure was equal over the entire surface of the water. When a vacuum was created at the top, the pressure on the water's surface was greater than the pressure inside the pipe, forcing the water inside it.

In spite of Torricelli's barometer and Boyle's experiments, many still had a difficult time accepting that air had weight. Boyle decided to conduct another experiment and conclusively prove that it did. He ordered a small glass bulb with a tiny tube that could be used to pump out air. He placed the bulb, sealed but full of air, on a balance scale inside the chamber of his air pump and put tiny weights on the scale to determine the weight of the glass bulb. Then he evacuated all of the air from the chamber, repeating the process until the balance of the glass bulb and weights was level. He then noted the weight of the glass bulb when it was full of air.

Next, Boyle pumped the air out of the glass bulb, sealed it, and placed it on the balance scale with the same amount of weight as before on the other side of the scale. As the air was again pumped out of the vacuum chamber, the side of the scale with the weights dropped. The bulb full of air had weighed more in the vacuum than the empty bulb had. He had proven conclusively that air had weight.

Boyle was preoccupied by the air's "spring," or compressibility, more than its weight. In 1660, he published his first book of scientific experiments, entitled *New Experiments in Physico-Mechanical: Touching the Spring of Air and its Effects*, widely known as *The Spring of Air*. Its goal, as Boyle wrote, was "to manifest, that the air hath a spring, and to relate some of its effects." In the book he describes the phenomenon we now refer to as air pressure. Boyle did not offer a definitive explanation of why air had pressure. However, he speculated that air might consist of particles similar to curls of wood or thin wires, which could be compressed but would bounce back when released.

The book detailed the results of forty-three numbered experiments using the air pump. Each number actually represented a series of experiments, which meant the book contained hundreds of experiments and results. Boyle wanted to provide exact details so others could duplicate his work. *The Spring of Air* was written in a straightforward style so non-scientists could read and understand it. In the spirit of the New Philosophy, one of the book's goals was to correct the entrenched ideas of Aristotle and the Peripatetic school.

The Spring of Air was an astonishing success. People all over Europe bought and read it. A London man named Samuel Pepys—whose famous diary serves as a sort of chronicle of the English Restoration, the period after Cromwell's death when the monarchy was restored in England—wrote about buying and reading it. He was so impressed he began attending meetings of the Invisible

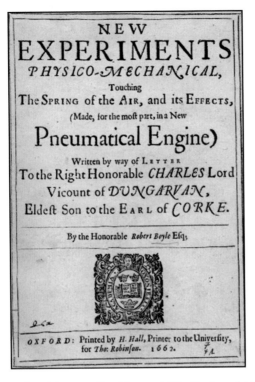

NEW
EXPERIMENTS
PHYSICO-MECHANICAL,
Touching
The Spring of the Air, and its Effects,
(Made, for the moft part, in a New
Pneumatical Engine)
Written by way of Letter
To the Right Honorable *CHARLES* Lord
Vicount of *DUNGARVAN*,
Eldeft Son to the Earl of *CORKE*.

By the Honorable *Robert Boyle* Efq;

OXFORD: Printed by *H. Hall*, Printer to the Univerfity,
for *Tho: Robinfon*. 1662.

The frontispiece of Boyle's groundbreaking work, The Spring of Air. (University of Leeds, England)

College. When Boyle visited London, Pepys assured him that he would buy every book that Boyle wrote.

The Spring of Air made Boyle one of the best-known scientists of his time. Although not all of Boyle's hypotheses on air were correct (for example, it is not true that air particles are literally shaped like springs), he had experimentally confirmed that air could be compressed and expanded. This was a major achievement. In the Aristotelian universe, air was, along with fire, the most mystical of the elements—elusive and intangible, but essential. Perhaps most importantly, by beginning the process of precisely identifying its properties and measuring its variables, *The Spring of Air* demystified air.

FOUR

boyle's law

Oliver Cromwell's death was an all-but-fatal blow to the English Protectorate. His son Richard, who succeeded him as Lord Protector, was an inexperienced and reluctant ruler. Only a year after his father's death, he abdicated under pressure from the army. Richard's abdication led to a brief, unstable period when Parliament ruled the country, but Royalist sentiment was on the resurgence and in May 1660 Parliament invited Charles II, who had been living in exile in Holland, to return and assume the throne. The Restoration period had begun.

The Boyle family had weathered the turmoil of revolution as well as anyone. Cromwell had needed the family's help in putting down the revolts in Ireland and had ignored their royalist sympathies. When it became clear the Protectorate was crumbling, two of Boyle's brothers had sent a letter to

Charles while he was still in Holland encouraging him to travel to Ireland and launch a campaign from there to seize the throne. It proved unnecessary to fight for the crown, but Charles II did not forget their loyal gesture; three of Boyle's brothers were awarded peerages.

The king also offered Boyle a title, and the Lord Chancellor offered him a high position in the Anglican Church, but he declined both honors. He felt that more titles and responsibilities would divert time and energy away from his experiments. Boyle did travel to London, however, for the festivities celebrating the king's return. The Restoration, known for its openness and extravagance, was an exciting time to be a wealthy gentleman in London. In contrast to the severe, overbearing Cromwell, Charles II, the so-called "Merry Monarch," was a fun-loving king who encouraged games and high society. Artists flourished and theaters, which had been banned under Cromwell, reopened, producing plays in a new, ribald genre called "Restoration comedy."

The new king was also an amateur scientist and attended several meetings of the Invisible College, which soon began calling itself the Royal Society of London for Improving Natural Knowledge. At an early meeting, King Charles viewed the heavens through a telescope. Boyle also demonstrated his experiments with the air pump for the king. In one performance he proved that two giant slabs of marble could be held together with air pressure.

During the later years of the Protectorate, the meetings of the Invisible College had become increasingly desultory

In 1667, one of the founders of the Royal Society of London, Thomas Sprat, published a book entitled the History of the Royal Society *which elaborated the scientific purposes of the academy and outlined some of the problems of scientific writing that set the modern standards for clarity and conciseness. This image, from the frontis of the book, depicts the president of the Royal Society and Francis Bacon sitting on either side of a bust of Charles II. In the background are a selection of scientific instruments, including an air pump. (From Sprat's* History of the Royal Society*)*

and were split between London and Oxford. Now its activity increased and the influential Sir Robert Moray reported that King Charles II approved of it. This motivated the members to write a charter, which Charles signed in 1662. In return for the royal charter, the Royal Society agreed to advise the king on scientific matters.

The Royal Society was a bastion of the New Philosophy. Its motto was "Nullius in Verba," Latin for "nothing by words." In other words, science can only be based on experiment and empirically verifiable fact, rather than on the untested ideas of ancient philosophers. The Royal Society still exists to this day and is an important funding agency for scientists throughout Britain and the world.

By the time Boyle returned to Oxford after the Restoration festivities, his high status, court favor, and the success of *The Spring of Air* had made him a national celebrity. He returned to his experiments and his writing, both of which accelerated as he hired new assistants, lab technicians, and secretaries.

All was not well, however. Boyle's eyesight, which had been deteriorating for some time, was now so poor he had a hard time writing his own manuscripts. He could see during the day, but under candlelight, "if I look upon somewhat distant objects, methinks I see them through a thin mist, or a little smoke," he wrote to a doctor friend. He tried several remedies of his own, including eyedrops of water, honey and crushed leaves, and dried manure blown into his eyes.

Despite his poor eyesight, Boyle continued working at a furious pace. He frequently traveled to London to participate in Royal Society meetings. The Society published thirty-five of his papers and performed numerous experiments at his suggestion. He donated his first air pump, now known as the *Machina Boylena*, to the Society as well as the services of his most valuable assistant, Robert Hooke, who became the Society's curator of experiments and went on to become one of the foremost scientists of the day, making important advancements in microscopy, biology, and architecture. Hooke even discovered and named the cell.

Boyle's high social standing and wealth lent the group a much-needed air of legitimacy. Despite the king's support, the Royal Society was not universally well-received by the academic establishment. Many professors and other salaried academics saw the New Philosophy as a direct rebuke to their own methods and ideas. Others regarded the Society as a threat to the university system, since it was not affiliated with any school.

Boyle published a prodigious amount of papers and books while living in Oxford. The sheer quantity of his work suggests that he served more as the head of a laboratory than as a hands-on experimentalist. He probably verified the experiments and helped to analyze the experimental data and draw the conclusions.

Boyle's most important book, however, did not comprise actual experiments, but instead gathered his thoughts about the scientific method. *The Sceptical Chymist,* published in 1661, is the book that many scientists think marked the beginning of modern chemistry. Boyle's goal in *The Sceptical Chymist* was to critically examine the methodology used in natural philosophy. "It is not so much my present

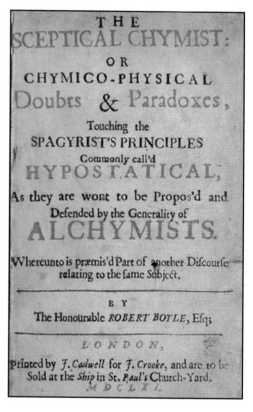

THE
SCEPTICAL CHYMIST:
OR
CHYMICO-PHYSICAL
Doubts & Paradoxes,
Touching the
SPAGYRIST'S PRINCIPLES
Commonly call'd
HYPOSTATICAL,
As they are wont to be Propos'd and
Defended by the Generality of
ALCHYMISTS.
Whereunto is præmis'd Part of another Discourse
relating to the same Subject.

BY
The Honourable ROBERT BOYLE, Esq;

LONDON,
Printed by J. Cadwell for J. Crooke, and are to be
Sold at the Ship in St. Paul's Church-Yard.
MDCLXI.

In his 1661 masterpiece, The Sceptical Chymist, Boyle appealed to fellow scientists to use experimentation in their work. (Courtesy of the Granger Collection.)

task to make assertions as to raise doubt," he wrote. A sceptic, now spelled skeptic, is a person who doubts and questions conventional wisdom. The book is written in the form of a philosophical dialogue among several friends, each of whom is a proponent of a different school. They gather at the home of Carneades, the skeptic.

One friend, Theimistius, is a Peripatetic. He fulsomely praises the beauty and elegance of Aristotle's system and refers to a burning log as an example of Aristotle's four elements:

The *fire* discovers itself in the flame by its own light; the smoke, by ascending to the top of the chimney, and there readily vanishing into *air*, like a river loosing itself in the sea, sufficiently manifests to what element it belongs, and gladly returns. The *water*, in its own form, boiling and hissing at the ends of the burning wood, betrays itself to more than one of our senses; and the ashes by their weight, their fieriness, and their dryness, put it past doubt, that they belong to the element of *earth*.

Carneades points out that Theimistius and the Peripatetics have simply accepted Aristotle's theory and sought to fit their every observation into it, rather than critically evaluating it. If an observation did not conform to Aristotle's theory, the Peripatetics generally rejected it as a false observation.

"Therefore the Peripatetics have not been very solicitous to gather experiments to prove their doctrines, but, rather to illustrate them," Boyle wrote. And since their entire discipline seemed to rest on logic and argument, they had done "little more than wrangle, without clearing up any mystery of nature, or producing any useful or noble experiments."

Aristotle's theory of the four elements also held that fire would reduce any matter to simpler substances. Boyle knew this did not always hold true. For example, mixing and heating soda ash, limestone, and sand produced glass, a more complex substance than the original ingredients. If the glass is heated, it melts, but it does not return to soda ash, limestone, and sand.

Another character in *The Sceptical Chymist*, Philoponus, followed the teachings of Paracelsus, a famous sixteenth-century alchemist. Paracelsus had rejected Aristotle's four

ALTERIVS NON SIT, QVI SVVS ESSE POTEST.

OMNE DONVM PERFECTVM A DEO, IMPERE A DIABO.

LAVS DEO, PAX VIVIS, REQVIES ÆTERNA SEPVLTIS.

ZOTH

AVREOLVS PHILIPPVS THEOPHRASTVS.

Early sixteenth-century alchemist and astrologer Paracelsus pioneered the use of chemicals and minerals in the developing field of medicine. (Courtesy of the Granger Collection.)

elements and said that that all matter was composed of salt, sulfur, and mercury and that only fire could reduce any compound material to one of the three elements. Carneades points out that this system is just as arbitrary as that of the Aristotelians. When alchemists wanted to reach a certain result, they would simply redefine their three principles in different ways. Because their experiments were shrouded in such secrecy and mysticism, they allowed themselves to get away with sloppy reasoning and conclusions:

> I fear that the chief reason, why chymists [alchemists] have written so obscurely of their three principles, may be, that not having clear and distinct notions of them themselves, they cannot write otherwise than confusedly of what they but confusedly apprehend: not to say, that divers of them, being conscious to the invalidity of their doctrine, might well enough discern, that they could scarce keep themselves from being confuted, but by keeping themselves from being clearly understood.

At least the alchemists endeavored to learn through experiments, as opposed to the Peripatetics. Boyle understood the value of experiments to test theories and that although a thousand successful experiments may confirm a theory, it only takes a single unsuccessful one to prove it invalid. Repetition is necessary before a scientist can rely on the results. Boyle often listed "several trials of the same thing, that they might naturally support and confirm one another." He also urged chemists to speak and write clearly about their experiments, successes, and failures.

The Sceptical Chymist attempted to drive a final stake into the heart of the Peripatetic way of studying the natural world, yet there was nothing new about Boyle's ideas. His insistence on induction and experimentation had precedents in the works of Galileo and Francis Bacon, and the Royal

Society had long held the Peripatetic school in contempt. But Boyle's enormous popularity ensured that the New Philosophy would thereafter be taken seriously.

Boyle also used *The Sceptical Chymist* to put forth his theory of matter, which he thought squared with the experiments recorded in *The Spring of Air*. Boyle advocated a corpuscular theory of matter—that all matter was composed of sub-units called corpuscles, which is somewhat similar to our modern conception of atoms or molecules. Boyle thought all objects were composed of a nearly infinite number of solid corpuscles that were separated in space. Corpuscles, which were flexible, allowed objects to be divided and to expand and contract, and diverse combinations of corpuscles explained the different observable properties of matter. Chemical reactions were simply changes in an object caused by the movement of individual corpuscles.

Boyle's corpuscular hypothesis was not the only alternative to Aristotle in circulation at the time. There was Decartes' theory of vortices, which had many adherents. Boyle did not adopt the Cartesian vortices, but he did believe that all physical phenomena could be explained by physical causes, a philosophy that came to be known as "mechanism."

Another prominent mechanist was the British political philosopher Thomas Hobbes, who is best remembered for his pessimistic treatise on government and the social contract, *Leviathan*. Hobbes thought the universe consisted of tiny particles, known as atoms, that moved about in a void. This was not a new idea—ancient Greek and Roman philosophers like Democritus, Epicurus, and Lucretius had all proposed versions of the same thing. The atomists claimed that the movement and behavior of all matter was due to the random collisions and interactions of these minuscule atoms.

Atomism had fallen out of vogue after Aristotle rejected it. However, by the time Boyle published the first editions of *The Spring of Air* and *The Skeptical Chymist*, the atomic hypothesis was in the midst of a renaissance. In 1642, a French physicist named Pierre Gassendi had written a book, based in part on Evangelista Torricelli's observations, arguing for atomism and proposing that atoms hooked together to form what he called molecules. Hobbes, a philosopher and mathematician, had proposed a similar hypothesis, which he claimed he had arrived at deductively.

Boyle distanced himself from the atomists, who were often considered to be atheists. If all physical phenomena were due to random chance and moving atoms, what about the will of God? Boyle's corpuscular theory was something of a compromise. Corpuscles were ill-defined, not nearly as specific as atoms, and his acceptance of the mechanistic idea that every physical action has a physical cause allowed him to avoid endorsing atomism. Boyle, a true skeptic, generally shied away from devising or endorsing grand systems that explained the entire universe, such as those proposed by Aristotle and Descartes.

The discussion about mechanism, atomism, and the

movement of atoms occasionally grew heated and even led to a clash between Boyle and Thomas Hobbes. Shortly after the publication of *The Spring of Air*, Hobbes, who scorned the New Philosophy and carried on a notorious rivalry with Boyle's friends Seth Ward and John Wallis, wrote a vicious response to it. Hobbes claimed that he had come to the same conclusions about air mathematically and questioned the necessity of experimentation.

Another critic of Boyle's was Franciscus Linus, a Jesuit professor at the University of Liège. Linus was an Aristotelian who objected to Boyle's experiments mainly because they did not fit the Aristotelian paradigm. It is fortunate for science that these men criticized Boyle's work, because it was in response to their criticisms that Boyle spelled out the theory that would later bear his name. In the second edition of *The Spring of Air*, published in 1662, Boyle responded to Hobbes's and Linus's criticisms with new experiments and also articulated what came to be known as Boyle's Law.

In these new experiments Boyle used his wealth to an advantage. He had a seventeen-foot-tall, J-shaped glass tube built. With the short end of the J sealed shut, he had mercury poured into the top of the tube while he stayed at the bottom and measured the height of the mercury collecting in the short leg. When enough mercury was poured in, and a pocket of air was trapped in the end of the short leg, he recorded the size of the air pocket and the height of the mercury in the long side. He found that when double the amount of mercury was poured into the long side, the air pocket shrank to half its earlier size. If the mercury was tripled, the air squeezed down to one-third its original size.

The experiment confirmed Boyle's earlier observations that air alone can support the weight of a significant amount of mercury and that air has an elastic quality. As the pressure from the mercury increased, the air pocket shrank. But when some mercury was removed, the air pocket expanded—just like a spring does when compressed and released. "The air was so compressed, as to be crowded into less than a quarter of the space that it possessed before," Boyle wrote.

More importantly, Boyle realized there was a mathematical relationship between the volume of the air pocket and the pressure put on it by the column of mercury, which led him to the principle that the volume of air is inversely proportional to its pressure. As pressure increases, volume shrinks. As pressure decreases, volume expands.

Boyle was cautious to limit his newly discovered principle, which came to be known as Boyle's Law, to air. He had not tested other gases and did not know if they would behave the same way. Later, experiments by others discovered that the law applies to all gases. The modern practical applications of Boyle's Law are manifold. By increasing pressure, large amounts of oxygen can be stored in relatively small metal containers for use in hospitals and for such activities as space flight and scuba diving. Welders use cylinders of compressed gases to fuel their torches.

For example, Boyle's Law is critical to scuba divers. If

a person dives without scuba gear, the amount of gas in his lungs stays the same, but its volume decreases under the pressure found deep underwater. When a diver uses a tank and regulator, the regulator keeps the air at the same pressure as the surroundings. A diver may be breathing air at the pressure equivalent of four atmospheres. Then, when divers ascend, they must remember to breathe out regularly. The air in their lungs is expanding in volume as the pressure around them decreases. If they do not equalize the pressure by expelling some of the air, the alveoli (small sacks in the lungs) may burst.

Any person who has flown on an airplane or driven up a steep mountain has probably experienced Boyle's Law at work. Higher up in the atmosphere, the air has lower pressure. As the person ascends, the air around his head is thinner than the air inside his head. To relieve the pressure, his ears will pop. Often, the ears will also pop as he descends and the pressure outside increases.

Fifteen years after Boyle published the second edition of *The Spring of Air*, a French scientist named Edme Mariotte independently discovered and announced the same law. Mariotte refined the principle by pointing out that temperature must remain constant in order for the relationship to hold true. In continental Europe, the law is known as Mariotte's Law.

About one hundred years after Boyle's experiments, a Frenchman named Jacques Alexandre César Charles observed a relationship between the temperature and the volume of a gas. As a gas is heated, its volume expands.

When the temperature falls, so does the volume. Charles never published a paper describing this phenomenon, but it is known as Charles's Law. In 1802, Joseph Gay-Lussac researched the relationship between temperature and pressure and discovered that they, too, are directly proportional to one another. This law was named for Gay-Lussac.

Taken together, Boyle's Law, Charles's Law and Gay-Lussac's Law are known as the ideal gas law in chemistry. Every beginning chemistry student learns the ideal gas law and how to use it to predict volume and pressure in experiments.

Boyle used the corpuscular hypothesis to explain the law. He thought the corpuscles coiled up when pressure increased and uncoiled when it decreased. Today we understand that gases are mixtures of individual particles called molecules. Air is a mixture of several gases, including nitrogen, oxygen, carbon dioxide, and water vapor. The molecules in air or in any other gas are constantly in motion. In between the molecules, there is empty space, a void, as Gassendi had suggested. If the pressure is increased, the space between the molecules grows smaller and the volume decreases. If the pressure is lowered, the molecules spread out and the volume expands.

chemical analysis

Many people were mystified by Boyle's decision to keep a small apartment in Oxford and live the life of a scholar when he could easily have assumed a title or taken up any number of the high honors offered to him. He was offered Henry Wotton's old job as the provost of Eton and was asked to be the president of the Royal Society. Boyle turned down both positions, the latter because the oath of office included statements of religious faith that did not match his beliefs. He did remain an active member of the Society until his death, however, and frequently presented experiments and demonstrations at meetings.

Boyle did not eschew all engagements outside of his scientific work. He financed several projects translating the Bible into Arabic, Malayan, Turkish, and Gaelic and

The house (center, with ladder) *in which Boyle lived on High Street was directly adjacent to Oxford's University College.* (Museum of the History of Science, Oxford)

donated large sums to help Irish peasants. He toyed with the idea of starting a monastic college in Ireland. King Charles appointed Boyle as governor of the Company for the Propagation of the Gospel in New England. The company's mission was to convert Native Americans living in New England to Christianity. Boyle took his position very seriously, not only donating money but also corresponding with many of the leaders in the colonies.

John Winthrop, the governor of the Massachusetts Bay Colony, wrote to Boyle asking if it was possible for a lightning bolt to strike a pond and kill all the fish as the Native Americans claimed. William Penn, the Quaker founder of Pennsylvania, described native American plants and flowers in letters to Boyle. Boyle also supported and corresponded with the Puritan missionary John Eliot.

Boyle served on the board of directors of the British East India Company, which had been formed eighty years earlier under the auspices of the Crown to establish lucrative trade with India and islands in the Indian Ocean. The company's ships carried cargoes of spices, silks, and gems to England. Boyle persuaded the company associates to promote the spread of Christianity wherever they traded and also asked company representatives to make observations and gather specimens for him. He recorded their findings in a notebook he entitled "Outlandish Book" and listed such phenomena as "perfume from a dung hill," odd diseases, and plant and animal life that were different from anything seen in England. He also asked his observers to note the stars, the temperature, the clarity of the air and water, and details about the people of each area.

Boyle expanded the scope of his scientific inquiries beyond air and gases. Together with Hooke, Christopher Wren, and Thomas Willis, the doctor who had initially recommended that Boyle hire Hooke, Boyle studied the circulation of blood. The group decided to inject a dose of opium—a narcotic that was often used to dull the senses and relieve pain—into a dog's leg. They discovered that liquids travel to the brain much more quickly and have a greater effect when administered intravenously rather than orally; after a few moments, the dog passed out. After reviving the groggy dog, the four eminent scientists took him to the garden and chased him around for a few hours to prevent him from falling into a coma. The dog recovered and became famous in England.

Boyle turned his attention to measuring heat and cold. Galileo had designed an early thermometer in 1606 that was an empty, open-ended tube connected to a column of colored water. As the temperature rose around the top of the tube, the air would expand and the water level would drop. When the temperature dropped, the air contracted, causing the water column to rise, much like the mercury in Torricelli's barometer. Ironically, Galileo's primitive version of the thermometer worked because of Charles's law, which would not be discovered for another 150 years. The thermometer had problems, however. In addition to changes in temperature, it also responded to changes in atmospheric pressure; also, if the temperature fell too far, the water would freeze. Unlike Galileo's thermometer, most subsequent thermometers work because of expanding liquid rather than expanding air.

Boyle designed a new thermometer that was a sealed glass tube filled with colored alcohol, most of which was held in a glass bulb at the bottom. When the heat rose and the alcohol expanded, it was forced up into the narrow tube. The alcohol would not freeze as water did, and because the thermometer was sealed, it would not respond to changes in atmospheric pressure. The added color also made the level easier to see. Boyle experimented with a number of different thermometers, although he never perfected his design. Eventually, it was discovered that mercury worked better than alcohol.

Boyle also realized that thermometers needed to be standardized and given fixed points to measure temperature. He argued that there was a need for a standard measurement for cold, just as there was for weight, volume and time. About forty years later, a German physicist named Gabriel Fahrenheit established such a system, which is now known as the Fahrenheit scale. Twenty years after Fahrenheit, a Swiss astronomer named Anders Celsius developed a more systematic scale, which also bears his name. Water's freezing point is zero degrees Celsius, while one hundred degrees Celsius is its boiling point.

As far back as the 1660s, however, Boyle had proved that the boiling point of water is not fixed. He had placed

Opposite: *Boyle stands next to one of his many air pumps in this colorized eighteenth-century engraving.* (Courtesy of the Granger Collection.)

warm water in a container in his air pump. As the air was pumped out, the water began to boil, even though the temperature was well below what was normally required to make water boil. By reducing the air pressure, he had also reduced the boiling point of water.

Having improved on the design of the thermometer, Boyle began to experiment on heat and cold. He correctly speculated that cold was the result of the particles in the substance (which Boyle, of course, called corpuscles) slowing down, but other aspects of heat and cold puzzled him. Many of Boyle's quandaries may today seem trivial. For example, Boyle was perplexed by how ginger could feel so hot in a person's mouth, but show no rise in temperature on a thermometer.

It was frustrating to have to wait for a freezing day to study the effects of cold. Boyle, however, used salt to lower the freezing point of water so he could study ice in his lab. He experimented with other substances and found that some also lowered water's freezing point, but that salt had the most significant effect. Boyle used his salt and ice mixture to investigate the action of water as it freezes.

It had long been known that water could break a container when it froze, but no one was certain why. Boyle decided to fill the barrel of a gun with water, stop up each end, and put the gun barrel in his salt and ice mixture. When he checked after two hours, the water was frozen and had cracked the metal gun barrel.

Most believed that all substances contract when they freeze. Others argued that even if most substances contract as they freeze, water is an exception and has to expand. Boyle accepted the latter theory and wanted to prove it. He filled a jar half full of water and placed it in a bucket. The bucket had a salt and ice mixture on the bottom and only ice around the top of the jar, causing the bottom to be much colder. The water in the jar froze from the bottom up and pushed out of the jar as it expanded.

Boyle had experimentally proven that water expands as it freezes. He measured the amount of expansion and found that water fills nine percent more space as ice than it does as a liquid. He also noted that ice floats and the tops of ponds freeze first, protecting the fish in the pond. Today we know that ice floats because its density is less than that of water, which is due to ice's crystalline structure. The molecules of ice arrange themselves in a lattice with a lot of empty space between the atoms, leading to its expansion and lighter density.

Since Aristotle's time, people had believed that hot water freezes faster than cold water. Boyle disproved this notion by putting out bowls of cold, warm, and hot water on a freezing day. He noted that they all froze at about the same time.

As he had before, Thomas Hobbes objected to Boyle's experiments and conclusions. Hobbes claimed that water froze first on the top of a pond because the wind blowing across it coagulated those parts first. Boyle disproved Hobbes by pumping a bellows and blowing air across a bowl of water for an extended time. No ice formed. In fact, Boyle noted that the water was not even cool.

Although most of the seventeenth century's most significant discoveries on light and optics would be made by Christiaan Huygens and Isaac Newton, Boyle spent some time studying light and published a book on the subject in 1664. *Experiments and Considerations Touching Colours* made a number of important observations, and may have influenced Newton. Boyle rejected the notion that color was an innate quality of all objects. He pointed out that blowing on an eyeball can cause a person to see colors, as can coughing or illness, and that prisms and films of oil on glass reveal a spectrum of light. The Peripatetics said these were not real but were illusions. Boyle countered that everything perceived by the sense organs—whether it be the sound of an echo or the sight of a rainbow—must be given its due importance. We now know that white light—that is, light from the sun—consists of a number of different types of light from throughout the electromagnetic spectrum. When held up to a prism, this white light is stratified into its constituent parts.

In the section of *Experiments and Considerations Touching Colours* that dealt with "whiteness and blackness," Boyle detailed experiments demonstrating that white objects reflect more light than other objects. Conversely, black objects—which tend to grow hot in the sunlight, he observed—absorb light. He speculated that the corpuscles on the surface of white bodies where spherically shaped, like tiny convex mirrors, so that they reflected the maximum amount of light. Black surfaces, on the other hand, were composed of irregular protuberances that reflected the light inward.

Boyle's work on color was emblematic of his dedication to the scientific method. He was not content to simply look at a black object and claim that it possessed some inherent quality of "blackness." He wanted to understand the specific mechanical processes that changed light in such a way that his eyes perceived black.

Boyle brought this same probing, rigorous approach to other chemical problems. In Boyle's time, the definition of acids and bases was peculiarly circular. If a substance bubbled when added to a base, it was said to be an acid. If a substance bubbled when added to an acid, it was said to be a base. This created some obvious problems. For instance, when vinegar was added to baking soda, it bubbled. But seventeenth-century scientists had no way of knowing which was the acid and which was the base. Boyle decided to look for a better way to define and detect acids and bases.

In the course of his experiments with color, Boyle had noticed that syrup of violets changed color in the presence of different chemicals. This phenomenon had been noticed before, but Boyle showed how it could be useful to chemists. The syrup turned red when mixed with known acids, such as vinegar or lemon juice, and green in the presence of known bases such as ammonia. Boyle decided to define substances as either acids or bases based on their reaction to violet syrup.

Soon thereafter, Boyle discovered another more enduring

test for alkalinity. He soaked a strip of paper in a solution of litmus, a material consisting of ground-up lichens, and dried out the strip. He found that the strip changed color when he put it into an acidic or basic solution. An acid would turn it red and a base would turn it blue. Litmus paper is still used in modern chemistry laboratories, and "litmus test" has entered the English lexicon as a term to denote a test with only two possible outcomes.

Boyle recognized that experiments can fail because of the impurity of ingredients, and he wanted to be able to precisely identify the different components of any given substance. He developed tests to identify copper and silver as well as the presence of salt and other various minerals in water. In fact, Boyle coined the term "chemical analysis," the investigation of the constituent parts of matter. Boyle had given chemists a term that described their mission in understanding matter.

Even when Boyle misunderstood the significance of his experiments and observations (he erroneously claimed, for instance, that he had transmuted water into earth through distillation), he always maintained that whatever he had witnessed had a material cause. He wrote a highly influential treatise, published in 1666, called *Origins of Forms and Qualities*, in which he fully articulated his mechanistic, corpuscular hypothesis.

He also argued against the Aristotelian "doctrine of forms," which held that any given object appears and acts the way it does because it is associated with a "form"—a sort of idealized version of the same object that possesses all of its corresponding properties. For Boyle, as a materialist, any explanation of an object's appearance or behavior had to address specific physical and mechanical causes. This idea may seem self-evident today, but it was revolutionary for the seventeenth century, and it underpinned almost every subsequent advance in western science.

SIX

plague and fire

In 1665, Boyle became embroiled in a controversy over a healer named Valentine Greatraks. Like Boyle, Greatraks was an Anglo-Irishman of considerable wealth. In 1662, he had "had an Impulse, or a strange perswasion [sic] in my [his] own mind" that he could cure scrofula, a variant of tuberculosis, by stroking victims with his hands. He tried out his newfound talent on a boy with the disease, who, whether by coincidence or design, recovered within a month. Greatraks traveled about Ireland and England, stroking the afflicted. Some claimed he was a savior; others thought he was a fraud.

A friend of Boyle's named Dr. Henry Stubb wrote Boyle a letter about Greatraks in which he commended the Irish Stroker, as Greatraks came to be known, comparing his powers and achievements to those of Jesus and the Apostles. The deeply religious Boyle took offense at this comparison but did not dismiss the possibility that Greatraks could heal.

Stubb had suggested that Greatraks healed by emitting an "effluvium"—a vague sort of vapor or emanation—onto those he stroked. Boyle responded, "what you say of the subtlety of the effluvia, and of the great efficiency they are capable of, will not be much struck at by a Corpuscularian." Boyle thought that the action and movements of invisible corpuscles could explain Greatraks's powers. He later attended one of Greatraks's healing sessions and personally attested to its validity. It may seem odd that one of the leaders of the Scientific Revolution should substantiate the highly suspect dealings of a mystical healer. But Boyle stuck to his mechanistic and corpuscular principles. He refused to believe that things simply "happened" without a specific, mechanical cause—in this case, an effluvium.

Boyle stayed in London for prolonged periods to attend Royal Society meetings and call on friends. He often stayed with his sister and even considered moving to London permanently. During one such stay, however, Boyle was forced to hastily return to Oxford.

London was no longer safe. Dutch merchant ships brought bubonic plague to England. The plague, known as the "Black Death," had killed one-third of Europe's population during the fourteenth century, and once again posed a large potential threat to England. When the disease reappeared with the merchant ships in 1664, it went

Several public health efforts were made during the Great Plague of London. Authorities ordered fires to be kept burning night and day, in hopes that the air would be cleansed. Substances giving off strong odors, such as pepper and hops, were also burned to ward off the infection. London residents, including young children, were urged to smoke tobacco. This contemporary woodcut depicts some of the chaos and despair. (Courtesy of the Granger Collection.)

virtually unnoticed for months, kept at bay by an especially cold winter. By the spring of 1665, however, incidences of plague began to crop up in London and by summer the disease was out of control. During the month of July, more than thirty thousand people died.

Highly infectious, the plague caused raging fever and black bumps and sores. The narrow, overcrowded streets were breeding grounds for rats, which carried the disease. People tried to contain it by marking red crosses on the doors of the infected, effectively quarantining them. Fires burned at all hours in an attempt to cleanse the air, but the disease spread, often killing whole families within a few days.

Wealthy people fled London to stay with relatives in the country or rented accommodations in nearby towns. Charles II removed to Oxford with his court, as his father had done during the English Civil War. Lady Ranelagh stayed with another sister in a nearby town.

The members of the Royal Society scattered throughout the country. Robert Hooke, William Petty, and John Wilkins packed up what scientific equipment they could and fled the city. Christopher Wren left for Paris. The young Isaac Newton left college and returned to his home in Woolthorpe.

Of the Royal Society, only Samuel Pepys, the man who kept a daily diary, and Henry Oldenburg, who was then the Society's secretary, remained in London. Oldenburg's letters to the scattered Society members described the smells of death and garbage everywhere and the desertion of parts of the city. Plague doctors roamed the streets, diagnosing the disease. When Boyle urged him to flee, Oldenburg answered that his responsibility was to care for the Royal Society's manuscripts. He bundled up the papers and placed them in storage in the basement of the famous St. Paul's Cathedral, where he felt sure they would be secure in the event that he caught the plague and died.

When the cooler weather of autumn arrived, the death tolls from the plague began to dwindle. Over 75,000 people had died, about one-fifth of London's population. By

This nineteenth-century etching imagines diarist and Royal Society member Samuel Pepys walking the streets of London under heavy garb during the Great Plague. (Courtesy of the Granger Collection.)

February 1666, King Charles II had returned, and most of the members of the Royal Society had also returned and went back to work on their experiments. Their weekly meetings resumed. Then, just as a sense of normalcy was beginning to return to London, another calamity struck.

Late on September 2, 1666, a fire broke out in a bakery on Pudding Lane in central London. The king's baker, Thomas Farynor, had accidentally left his ovens burning overnight. At some point during the night, a spark from the ovens leapt onto a stack of nearby firewood. High winds swept more sparks onto nearby buildings, setting them ablaze. The night watchman notified the Lord Mayor of London, who came to have a look and decided the fire would burn itself out when it reached the River Thames. But when it reached the river the next morning, the fire instead gathered fuel from the warehouses of oil, pitch, lumber, and coal that lined the riverbank and grew into an unstoppable inferno.

The firestorm raced along both banks of the river, leaping into nearby streets and spreading from one wooden, thatched-roof house to the next. Firefighters tried to stop it by pulling down buildings in its path. When the blaze jumped over those fire lanes, they used gunpowder to blast even bigger swaths to deny the fire fuel to burn. A shift in the wind took the fire in another direction; for three days, the fire burned out of control.

When it finally died down, the fire was recognized as the worst disaster in the history of London. Seventy-five percent of the old walled city was destroyed and tens of thousands lost their homes. To a population already devastated by the plague, the fire seemed like a judgment from God on the excesses of the Restoration era.

Among the ninety churches that burned was St. Paul's, where Oldenburg had stored the Royal Society's manuscripts

and records. Many had thought the large stone building would withstand the blaze. Booksellers in the nearby neighborhood had brought books from their shops and stored them alongside the Royal Society's papers in the basement. Unfortunately, the roof of St. Paul's consisted of lead sheets supported by wooden timbers. On the third day, the timbers began to burn and the heat was so intense that the leaden roof melted and ran into the basement, setting the precious books and manuscripts on fire.

In the aftermath of the disastrous fire, King Charles called on the members of the Royal Society to help rebuild the city in their capacity as his science advisers. Christopher

Wren, who was a consummate architect, was appointed to head the effort. Wren told his fellow Royal Society members that he planned to design a city with wider streets and homes made of brick, which could withstand fire. Robert Hooke served as Wren's chief assistant and as surveyor to the City of London. Together, they also redesigned St. Paul's Cathedral, which is now one of the most splendid churches in England.

When Boyle told his sister about the plan for a redesigned London, she objected. She felt that the city leaders needed to rebuild the city as quickly as possible. When Boyle asked why, she took him on a tour of a field north of town. Hundreds of thousands of Londoners were living

Christopher Wren's plans for the redesign of St. Paul's Cathedral were rejected twice before they were finally accepted in 1675. The cathedral was finished in 1708, and Wren was the first person to be interred there, in 1723. (British Library)

in a tent colony. Their homes had been destroyed in the fire, forcing them to live in tents until the houses were rebuilt. Boyle realized these people needed his help and gave large sums of money to aid the victims.

From 1666 to 1668, Boyle traveled frequently between his apartment in Oxford and his sister's house in London. He contemplated moving in with her permanently, but he was still attached to his friends and laboratory in Oxford.

During these years he continued to experiment and to write. The phenomenon of bioluminescence fascinated Boyle. Some fungi and bacteria glow, or luminesce, naturally. Boyle used his air pump to show that the process required air. As with combustion and respiration, bioluminescence was later proven to require oxygen.

By 1668, Katherine's husband had died and Boyle's reasons to relocate to London were growing. He was forty-one years old and had recurring malaria, which often sent him to bed with fever and chills. A slender and frail man, he kept a selection of cloaks of different weights to stay warm in various environments. Since his twenties, Boyle had suffered from what he thought was a kidney stone. His eyes continued to bother him, making it difficult to read or write, and he dictated letters and manuscripts to his assistants and had them read correspondence and scientific news to him.

Boyle decided to move to London to live with his sister. Katherine lived on Pall Mall, a main thoroughfare in London that had been untouched by the Great Fire. It was a pleasant neighborhood full of spacious houses and nice shops.

A seventeenth-century view of Pall Mall, the London neighborhood where Boyle lived with his sister from 1668 until his death. (Courtesy of the Granger Collection.)

Stretching along one side of the neighborhood were the Royal Gardens and St. James's Park, where King Charles would release exotic animals sent to him from around the world. The area set a trend in neighborhood design with rows of storefronts lining the streets. Shopkeepers began calling these areas shopping malls.

When Boyle moved to London, Katherine set aside a section of her house for his laboratory, but he worked in cramped quarters compared to his laboratory in Oxford. He even kept some chemical equipment in his bedroom. More than three thousand books were unloaded from wagons and hauled to his rooms, along with crates of glassware, instruments, and chemicals. His latest air pump was also installed in his laboratory. Robert Hooke helped his former mentor set up the equipment and arrange the laboratory.

Boyle hired new assistants and resumed his experiments. He was still preoccupied with combustion. Using a device known as a burning glass, which focused rays of the sun onto a single point, like a magnifying glass, he tried to burn various materials in the chamber of his air pump. But the burning glass was of limited use. The glass sides of the chamber scattered some of the rays so that only highly combustible substances would ignite. Also, it only worked on sunny days. Boyle devised an alternative. He heated a metal plate to a red-hot temperature and placed it in the bottom of the chamber. He could then hang his material of choice by a fine wire attached to the top of the chamber. The heat from the plate caused most materials to ignite.

As with the candle in the air pump, Boyle found that his vacuum snuffed out most combustion. But he got a surprise when he tested gunpowder, which is composed of sulfur, charcoal, and saltpeter, or potassium nitrate. When heated on the hot plate in air, the gunpowder exploded, as Boyle expected. But when he pumped the air out of the chamber and reheated the gunpowder, it burned in the vacuum (although it did not explode). Curious, he devised another experiment. He filled a goose quill with gunpowder, lit it, and submerged it in water. The gunpowder burned, giving off smoky bubbles. Boyle decided that whatever component of air allowed combustion was also present in gunpowder. Today we know that substance to be oxygen, present in air and bound up in the potassium nitrate part of gunpowder.

Katherine and Boyle, who was at the height of his celebrity, entertained frequently in their home on Pall Mall. Henry Oldenburg lived nearby and visited often, as did Robert Hooke. Another neighbor was Isaac Barrows, a gifted mathematician, preacher, and charter member of the Royal Society. Barrows had taught at Trinity College, Cambridge, but had given up his chair to become King Charles's chaplain. Barrow's pupil, Isaac Newton, took his place at Trinity.

Boyle also received international visitors, including the Grand Duke of Tuscany. Boyle regaled the duke with demonstrations of the air pump, experiments with colors, and a model of the moon.

In the midst of experiments and entertaining, Boyle's health worsened. Throughout his life, he had fought health problems with concoctions from his own laboratory. He would mix herbs and powders for all types of ailments, often trusting his own medicines more than those of doctors. Some friends even accused him of being a hypochondriac. William Petty, the physician Boyle had studied under while in Ireland, once teased Boyle, "The next disease you labour under is your apprehension of many diseases, and a continual fear, that you are always inclining or falling into one or another." But Boyle's most serious health crisis was still yet to come.

SEVEN

poor health

In 1670, Boyle suffered a debilitating stroke. For a week, his friends and family prepared for the worst; most people who suffered strokes did not survive. Boyle's friend John Evelyn reported that Boyle experienced "frequent attacks of palsies" and could not "bring his hand to his mouth." Already a stutterer, Boyle's speech became even slower and more halting. On good days, he instructed his assistants to perform experiments and then discussed the results with them.

Every day, Boyle had someone carry him outside to take fresh air. His assistants gave him regular foot and leg massages and helped him to exercise his hands and arms. He tried many laboratory remedies to help him recover, of which he found "the dried flesh of vipers seemed to be one of the most usefullest." After about eleven months, he had regained enough strength to leave his bed. He resumed his experiments and put on a demonstration for the Royal Society. Boyle believed that his faith in God had given him the strength to recover. In fact, he was able to write more books in the five years after his stroke than in the five years before.

In 1667, a German alchemist named Johann Daniel Kraft had attended a Royal Society meeting in London to show off a newly discovered material called phosphorus. Henning Brand, a fellow alchemist of Kraft's, had accidentally discovered the substance eight years earlier while distilling his urine in an attempt to make gold. For Kraft's demonstration, he closed all of the shutters and put out all of the lamps in the Royal Society's meeting place. Kraft produced a small glass vial containing a tiny piece of phosphorus, which glowed in the darkness. Hooke, who was in attendance, shook the vial and found that it "appeared to shine more vividly." When Kraft wrote on a piece of paper with the substance, the writing glowed so brightly it could be read from both sides of the paper. The word phosphorus, in fact, means "lightbearer."

Inspired by Kraft's demonstration and recovering his strength after the stroke, Boyle and his assistant Ambrose Godfrey Hanckwitz prepared and began experimenting with their own phosphorus. They tried to dissolve it in a number of liquids, such as water, turpentine, and oil. It could be ignited with a burning glass. Boyle published two books on his experiments with phosphorus. Hanckwitz later went

At age nineteen, Ambrose Godfrey Hanckwitz traveled to London from Saxony to assist Boyle in his work with phosphorus. After parting ways with Boyle, Hanckwitz went on to become an apothocary and manufacturer of phosphorus. (Smithsonian Institution Libraries, Washington, D.C.)

into business making the substance, and for forty years he was the largest phosphorus producer in Europe.

Today phosphorus is used in explosives, pesticides, detergents, and toothpaste. Boyle discovered one of the substance's most enduring practical applications. He coated a rough sheet of paper with phosphorus residue and then pulled a sulfur-tipped stick through a fold in the paper. The stick ignited; Boyle had designed the first match.

Boyle lived with his sister for more than twenty years. A visitor to his rooms commented, "Glasses, pots, chemical and mathematical instruments, books and bundles of papers, did so fill and crowd his bed-chamber, that there was but just room for a few chairs." He spent his mornings in private devotions and experimenting in his laboratory. In the afternoon, he received visitors.

Guests streamed to the house on Pall Mall to meet Boyle. At his sister's suggestion, he rented some rooms in another part of the city. When the strain of entertaining so many visitors became too great for him, he would retire to his secret lodgings and rest.

In 1680, Boyle published the second edition of *The Sceptical Chymist*, which contained a definition of elements that comes very close to the modern definition. "I now mean by elements," Boyle wrote, "certain primitive and simple, or perfectly unmingled bodies; which not being made of any other bodies, or of one another, are the ingredients, of which those called perfectly mixt bodies are immediately compounded, and into which they are ultimately resolved." Our definition of an element today is a substance that cannot be decomposed into other substances by chemical methods.

Although Boyle had lambasted the obscure practices of alchemists, he continued to attempt transmutation. He claimed to have produced a substance he called "red earth" that actually degraded gold into silver. His view that water could be transmuted into earth through distillation persisted until the eighteenth century, when the French chemist Antoine Lavoisier disproved it. Boyle also lobbied the English parliament to end a ban against multiplying silver and gold that had originally been instituted under Henry IV. The law was repealed in 1689.

It was, in fact, in Boyle's capacity as an alchemist that he exchanged his first correspondence with the younger Isaac Newton. In 1676, Boyle had sent a paper to the Royal Society claiming that he had purified mercury to the point where its constitution approached that of gold. Newton, who was also interested in alchemy, wrote to Boyle expressing his doubt about the discovery and pleading that "the great wisdom of the noble author will sway him to high silence till he shall be resolved of what consequence the thing may be."

Boyle did not heed Newton's warning, and in 1678 he published a short, uncharacteristically obscure dialogue describing the discovery. Boyle claimed to have delayed publishing his discovery for several years because he feared the corrupting effects of the unalloyed wealth that his elixir would produce.

While Boyle had been immersing himself in laboratory

Isaac Newton served as the president of the Royal Society from 1703 through 1727. He is widely considered one of the most influential scientists and mathematicians in history. (National Portrait Gallery, London)

work at Lady Ranelagh's house in London, England once again found itself in the midst of upheaval. In 1685, King Charles II, to the great consternation of most English Protestants, converted to Catholicism on his deathbed. His brother James, who was a known Catholic, succeeded him and soon began appointing Catholics to high positions in the government and universities.

In 1688, the birth of James's son stirred up fears of a Catholic dynasty in England. The Tories and the Whigs, the two main political parties in Parliament, united against the king. Several English nobles offered support if Mary, the estranged Protestant daughter of the king, and her Dutch husband William of Orange would come to England and depose James. William invaded with his army and James, who realized he did not have enough support to win an armed conflict, fled to France. William and Mary became the new king and queen of England. The bloodless overthrow of James II became known as the Glorious Revolution.

In 1688, when the religious divisions that would lead to the Glorious Revolution were still brewing, Boyle wrote a polemic against Roman Catholicism called *Protestant and Papist*. Although his prejudice against Catholics may today seem bigoted, what Boyle most objected to in Catholicism was the professed infallibility of the pope and the church. Boyle approached everything, from religion to science, with an astute skepticism. He distrusted entrenched dogmas, whether they were Aristotle's or the pope's.

Though Boyle's health continued to falter, he remained

Robert Boyle in 1689. (Courtesy of the Granger Collection.)

mentally active. His friend John Evelyn wrote of him:

> The contexture of his body . . . appeared to me so delicate that I have frequently compared him to a chrystal, or Venice glass; which, though wrought never so thin and fine, being carefully set up, would outlast the hardier metals of daily use. And he was withal as clear and candid; not a blemish or spot to tarnish his reputation.

In 1689, however, he took a turn for the worse. In his weakened state, he published a notice limiting his time for visitors to Tuesday and Friday mornings and Wednesday and Saturday afternoons so that he could have time to get his papers "into some kind of order, that they may not remain useless."

He continued to turn out books at an astonishing pace, considering his age and poor health. A number of his books foreshadowed Deism, a philosophy that would dominate the intellectual landscape of the European Enlightenment during the eighteenth century. Deists believed that all religion, including Christianity, is founded on a rational basis. *The Excellency of Theology, Compared with Natural Philosophy*, published in 1674, addressed the existence of God. "The vastness, beauty, orderliness, of the heavenly bodies; the excellent structure of animals and plants; and the other phenomena of nature," he wrote, "justly induce an intelligent and unprejudiced observer to conclude a supremely powerful, just, and good author."

Another book, *The Christian Virtuoso,* defended religion

and science and claimed that the two mutually reinforced one another. Boyle believed that the natural world was God's creation and that scientists served God by discovering the natural laws. He described the universe as a clock God had created and set into motion. The metaphor of God as a clockmaker was one that many subsequent Deists would use.

Boyle's *Medicina Hydrostatica,* published in 1690, discusses specific gravity. Each substance, Boyle wrote, has its own specific gravity—a ratio of its density in relation to that of another substance (usually water, but sometimes air). He also published the first account in England of the use of a hydrometer, a device used to measure specific gravity of liquids. The hydrometer consists of a sealed tube of mercury or lead that causes the vessel to float upright. The tube is placed inside a jar of the liquid in question. The point at which the surface of the liquid touches the tube indicates its specific gravity. The lower the density of the liquid, the lower the tube will sink. Hydrometers are still used today.

In July 1691 Boyle wrote out his will. He left money and gifts for his family and servants but donated a large portion of his estate to various charities, including the Company for the Propagation of the Gospel in New England. He left his minerals and instruments to the Royal Society. He also endowed a lecture series called the Boyle Lectures, which still continues to this day, for the purpose of "proving the Christian religion against notorious infidels, viz. Atheists, Theists, Pagans, Jews, and Mahometans, not

Both Robert and Katherine were buried at St. Martin-in-the-Fields. (British Library)

descending lower to any controversies, that are among Christians themselves."

Boyle, with his weak constitution, always felt that Katherine would outlive him even though she was almost thirteen years older than he was. When she died on December 23, 1691, he was devastated. He buried her in a cemetery at St. Martin-in-the-Fields church. Only eight days later, on December 31, he died in his sleep. He was sixty-four years old.

Boyle was interred next to his sister at St. Martin-in-the-Fields. The church was later torn down and replaced, and no record remains of where Boyle's body was moved. People across Europe mourned his death. "England has lost her wisest man, wisdom her wisest son, and all Europe the man whose writings they most desired," one friend wrote. An obituary read, "The Honorable Mr. Boyle . . . hath ended his life with the year, to the unspeakable loss of the learned."

EIGHT

legacy

Two days after Boyle's funeral, Samuel Pepys, who had recently served a two-year stint as the president of the Royal Society, invited a small group of friends to his house for a memorial service and tribute to Boyle. At the gathering, the men symbolically passed the mantle to Boyle's successor, Isaac Newton. This was an apt gesture, since it was Newton's ideas that would dominate science for the next 250 years. Newton, in his *Principia Mathematica*, described universal gravitation and the three laws of motion. He spawned an era when physicists and scientists sought to organize the universe by uncovering the laws and principles that controlled the diverse phenomena observed in nature.

A possibly more fitting bequest was made by Boyle himself. His papers were left in the care of a physician

Boyle left Enlightenment philosopher John Locke in charge of his papers when he died. (The Hermitage, St. Petersburg)

and political philosopher named John Locke, whom Boyle had superficially known in Oxford and through the Royal

Society. Boyle had hoped that Locke would simply set his affairs in order, but he did more than that. In 1710, Locke wrote *Treatise Concerning the Principles of Human Knowledge*, forming the bedrock of a school known as British Empiricism. The empiricists believed that the only way to discern truth was through a judicious combination of observation and logic. Under empiricism, the subsequent developments of European science flourished.

Boyle was not a philosopher of science of the same order as Galileo, Bacon, Descartes, or even Aristotle. His inductive method was the standard of the New Philosophy. Yet he changed the way scientific investigations were done. Boyle's wealth, universal regard, and fame helped change the way most people perceived experimentalists. If a man of noble birth like Robert Boyle was not above experimentation, who was? Boyle's accessible books mobilized a movement to modernize chemistry, bringing alchemists "out of their dark and smoky laboratories," as he put it. Boyle wanted to establish openness and accountability in science. This was only possible if scientists wrote up their work in clear, precise language and based all of their theories on rigorous, empirical tests.

If Boyle's biggest accomplishment was convincing people of the value of scientific experimentation, the knowledge gained from his experiments was also invaluable. Boyle's Law is a cornerstone of modern chemistry and physics. Its practical applications range

This engraving depicts the laboratory of Boyle's assistant, Ambrose Godfrey Hanckwitz, in 1707. Because no images or descriptions exist of Boyle's own lab, this illustration is thought to be one of the closest representations of what Boyle's well-equipped lab might have looked like. (City of Westminster Public Library, London)

from aerosol cans to scuba diving gear. He can also claim a number of inventions, including the match, the pressure cooker, and the litmus test.

The seventeenth century was an exciting and tumultuous time for science. The Aristotelian universe was beginning to unravel, and scientists scrambled to propose alternate theories—to "fill in the vacuum," so to speak. Their explanations were often as bizarre and unrealistic as the ones they replaced. For example, the Flemish alchemist Jan Baptist van Helmont, one of Boyle's early mentors, proposed that all matter was a variation of water, which was animated by different types of seeds.

As a general rule, Boyle avoided the type of premature speculation that characterized many of his scientific peers, and the corpuscular view that he advanced ultimately proved to be remarkably on target. Corpuscularianism evolved gradually into an atomic theory like that described by Pierre Gassendi. Today we know that the universe is, in fact, composed of atoms and molecules, whose interactions account for most chemical and physical phenomena. It is in some ways ironic that Boyle feuded with Thomas Hobbes, since both ultimately came to be associated with the ideas of mechanism, atomism, and materialism that would characterize scientific thinking in the eighteenth century.

Few scientists better represent the many contradictions of the age than Boyle. He abhorred Catholicism, yet also shunned the parochialism of many of his fellow Protestants. He derided the methods of alchemists, yet was a practitioner of alchemy. He was a mechanical corpuscularian, yet he attributed his own good fortune to the intervention of Divine Providence. In an age of transition, Robert Boyle was the ultimate man of transition.

timeline

1660	Publishes *New Experiments Physico-Mechanical: Touching the Spring of the Air.*
1661	Publishes *The Sceptical Chymist*, which marks the beginning of modern chemistry.
1662	Publishes second edition of *Spring of Air*, where he first publishes what comes to be known as Boyle's Law: as pressure on a gas increases, the gas takes up less volume.
1662	The Royal Society officially begins.
1664	Proves that water expands as it freezes. He also invents the litmus test to identify acids and bases.
1665	Plague strikes London. One-fifth of the population is killed.
1666	The Great Fire of London destroys much of the city.
1668	Moves to London to live with his sister because of his worsening health.
1670	Suffers a stroke.
1670s	Experiments with combustion and phosphorous; invents the match.
1680	Publishes second edition of *The Skeptical Chymist*.
1691	Dies in sleep on December 31.

sources

CHAPTER ONE: Privileged Son

p. 11, "by God's blessing . . ." Robert Boyle, "An Account of Philaretus during his Minority," in *The Works*, ed. Thomas Birch, (London, 1772; repr., Hildesheim: Georg Olms Verlagsbuchhandlung, 1965), 1:xii.

p. 13, "To be such parents' son . . ." Ibid., xiii.

p. 13, "Great men's children . . ." J. R. Jacob, *Robert Boyle and the English Revolution* (New York: B. Franklin, 1977), 8.

p. 13, "half a score," Boyle, "An Account of Philaretus," in *The Works*, 1:xiv.

p. 14, "God's province is . . ." Louis Trenchard More, *The Life and Works of the Honourable Robert Boyle* (New York: Oxford University Press, 1944), 17.

p. 14, "prefers learning above all . . ." R. E. W. Maddison, *The Life of the Honourable Robert Boyle, F.R.S.* (London: Taylor and Francis, 1969), 11.

p. 19, "so greedily in reading . . ." More, *Life and Works*, 28.

p. 19, "to fetter, or at least . . ." Ibid., 29.

p. 22, "was suddenly waked . . ." Ibid., xxii.

p. 22, "whereupon the consideration . . ." Ibid., 45.

p. 22, "deep raving melancholy," Ibid., 46.

CHAPTER TWO: Dilettante Scientist

p. 28, "she cried out . . ." Maddison, *Life of the Honourable Robert Boyle*, 53.

p. 29, "one of the most beautiful . . ." More, *Life and Works,* 54.

p. 32, "Never reveal clearly . . ." John Hudson Tiner, *Robert Boyle: Trailblazer of Science* (Milford, MI: Mott Media, 1989), 93.

p. 33, "into as many pieces as we . . ." More, *Life and Works*, 66.

p. 33, "I have been so unlucky . . ." Maddison, *Life of the Honourable Robert Boyle*, 70.

p. 33, "Vulcan [the Roman god of fire] . . ." Ibid., 71.

p. 34-35, "an observing native . . . of his country," More, *Life and Works*, 158.

p. 38, "It has been long . . ." Ibid., 68.

p. 39, "more of the variety . . ." Ibid., 76.

CHAPTER THREE: The Spring of Air

p. 45, "is sometimes heavier . . ." J. J. O'Connor and E. F. Robertson, "Evangelista Torricelli," MacTutor History of Mathematics, http://www-history.mcs.st-andrews.ac.uk/ Biographies/Torricelli.html (accessed July 6, 2006).

p. 47, "the bladder appeared as full . . ." Boyle, *New*

Experiments Physico-Mechanical touching the Spring of Air, in *The Works*, 1:18.

p. 47, "the bladder was proportionally . . ." Ibid.

p. 50, "For we see . . ." Ibid., 108.

p. 50-51, "To the Danish Agent . . ." John Gribbin, *The Scientists: A History of Science Told Through the Lives of its Greatest Inventors* (New York: Random House, 2002), 138.

p. 53 , "we assent to experience . . ." Ibid., 136.

p. 54, "nature had not so placed . . ." More, *Life and Works*, 179.

p. 56, "to manifest, that the . . ." Boyle, *Spring of Air*, in *The Works,* 1:12.

CHAPTER FOUR: Boyle's Law

p. 62, "if I look upon . . ." More, *Life and Works*, 108.

p. 63, "It is not so much . . ." Ibid., 245.

p. 64-65, "The *fire* discovers itself . . ." Ibid., 247.

p. 65, "Therefore the Peripatetics . . ." Ibid., 262.

p. 65, "little more than wrangle . . ." Rose-Mary Sargent, *The Diffident Naturalist: Robert Boyle and the Philosophy of Experiment* (Chicago: University of Chicago Press, 1995), 26.

p. 67, "I fear the chief reason . . ." More, *Life and Works*, 250.

p. 67, "several trials of . . ." Sargent, *The Diffident Naturalist*, 200.

p. 71, "the air was so compressed . . ." Boyle, "A Defense of Mr. Robert Boyle's Explications of his Physico-Mechanical Experiments Against Franciscus Linus," in *The Works*, 1:159.

CHAPTER FIVE: Chemical Analysis

p. 76, "perfume from a dung hill," Boyle, "Experiments and Observations about the Mechanical Production of Odours," in *The Works*, 4:271.

CHAPTER SIX: Plague and Fire

p. 86, "had an Impulse . . ." Maddison, *Life of the Honourable Robert Boyle*, 123.

p. 87, "what you say of the . . ." More, *Life and Works*, 123.

p. 97, "The next disease you labour . . ." Ibid., 77.

CHAPTER SEVEN: Poor Health

p. 98, "frequent attacks of palsies . . ." More, *Life and Works*, 130.

p. 98-99, "the dried flesh of vipers . . ." Ibid., 131.

p. 99, "appeared to shine . . ." Maddison, *Life of the Honourable Robert Boyle*, 159.

p. 101, "Glasses, pots, chemical . . ." Ibid., 187.

p. 101, "I now mean by elements . . ." Boyle, *The Sceptical Chymist*, in *The Works*, 1:562.

p. 102, "the great wisdom . . ." More, *Life and Works*, 216.

p. 106, "The contexture of his body . . ." Gribbin, *The Scientists*, 142.

p. 106, "into some kind of order . . ." Maddison, *Life of the Honourable Robert Boyle*, 177.

p. 106, "The vastness, beauty . . ." More, *Life and Works*, 184.

p. 107, "proving the Christian religion . . ." Ibid., 132.

p. 109, "England has lost . . ." Maddison, *Life of the Honourable Robert Boyle*, 188.

p. 109, "The Honorable Mr. Boyle . . ." Ibid., 191.

CHAPTER EIGHT: Legacy

p. 112, "out of their dark and . . ." Boyle, *The Sceptical Chymist*, in *The Works*, 1:461.

bibliography

Abbott, David, ed. *The Biographical Dictionary of Scientists: Chemists*. New York: Peter Bedrick Books, 1983.

Boerst, William J. *Galileo Galilei and the Science of Motion*. Greensboro: Morgan Reynolds Publishing, 2004.

————. *Isaac Newton: Organizing the Universe*. Greensboro: Morgan Reynolds Publishing, 2004.

Boyle, Robert. *The Skeptical Chemist*. Mineola, NY: Dover Publications, 2003.

————. *The Works*. Edited by Thomas Birch. London, 1772. Reprint, Hildensheim: Georg Olms Verlagsbuschhandlung, 1965.

Gribbin, John. *The Scientists: A History of Science Told Through the Lives of its Greatest Inventors*. New York: Random House, 2002.

Maddison, R. E. W. *The Life of the Honourable Robert Boyle, F.R.S.* London: Taylor and Francis, 1969.

More, Louis Trenchard. *The Life and Works of the Honourable Robert Boyle*. New York: Oxford University Press, 1944.

O'Connor, J. J. and E. F. Robertson. "Evangelista Torricelli." MacTutor History of Mathematics, http://www-history. mcs.st-andrews.ac.uk/Biographies/Torricelli.html.

Principe, Lawrence. *The Aspiring Adept: Robert Boyle and His Alchemical Quest.* Princeton, NJ: Princeton University Press, 1998.

Sargent, Rose-Mary. *The Diffident Naturalist: Robert Boyle and the Philosophy of Experiment.* Chicago: University of Chicago Press, 1995.

Tiner, John Hudson. *Robert Boyle: Trailblazer of Science.* Milford, MI: Mott Media, 1989.

web sites

The Boyle Project at Birkbeck College, University of London
http://www.bbk.ac.uk/boyle/boyle_papers/boylepapers_index.htm

The Stanford Encyclopedia of Philosophy
http://plato.stanford.edu/archives/sum2002/entries/boyle

Woodrow Wilson Leadership Program in Chemistry, The Chemical Heritage Foundation
http://www.chemheritage.org/classroom/chemach/forerunners/boyle.html

University College, Oxford
http://web.comlab.ox.ac.uk/oxinfo/univ-col/boyle-hooke.html

The MacTutor History of Mathematics, University of St. Andrew's, Scotland
http://www-groups.dcs.st-and.ac.uk/~history/index.html

index